Praise for *Take Back Your Home*

"Morgan is a master at turning big concepts into actionable steps. In *Take Back Your Home*, she shares experiences, tips, and guidelines in an approachable and thoughtful manner. Her writing connects with readers by breaking down complex ideas into easy-to-understand and implementable steps, making *Take Back Your Home* a must-read for anyone looking for real organizing strategies."

—**Jessica Litman**, author of *Home Sweet Organized Home* and host of the podcast *Organizing Tune-Ups*

"Reading one of Morgan's books makes it seem like you have your own personal professional organizer BFF right at your fingertips. Her blend of stories and practical down-to-earth advice draws you in, giving you the confidence to tackle your own clutter. She breaks down complicated tasks so it seems more manageable to create a life you love that is a lot less overwhelming and a lot more meaningful."

—**Bridget Stralko**, Detroit professional organizer and founder of Unclutter It

"Morgan's well-honed experience and commitment to helping you take back your home leaps off the pages of this book. She thoughtfully explains the process that she uses with her in-home clients. Now it's your turn to bring Morgan and her organization skills into your home. It will change your life."

—**Lisa Trigsted**, CEO and founder, Get Neat With Lisa

"Morgan's new book is filled with practical wisdom and implementable tips. Her personal experiences provide a foundation for the advice she gives the reader. Morgan is a great writer and gets straight to the point, which is good news for anyone looking to change their life—starting today!"

—**Diane Boden**, creator of the *Minimalist Moms Podcast*

"I never imagined working with someone like Morgan until my daughter made me. At that point, I'd moved across the country with the idea of reorganizing my life, and my daughter said I should start by reorganizing my living space. I lucked out with Morgan, who never forced some pre-set agenda on me, but instead got to know me as a person and adapted every suggestion to my unique preferences and patterns. For the first time in forever, I feel my home is a reflection of me as I wish to be."

—**Bill Slayton**, retired teacher

"In *Take Back Your Home*, Morgan Tyree not only provides insight into the myriad specialties within the Pro Organizing community, but also into the value and expertise imparted through Pro Organizers. Tyree shares her experience as a solopreneur Pro Organizer that goes above and beyond—giving consideration to life events which directly impact how you feel in your home. Tyree also shares the importance and necessary knowledge base which ultimately supports and keeps clients accountable in meeting their goals to live with less."

—**Dalys Macon**, professional organizer and founder of D'Vine Order

"Morgan's passion for helping others and her dedication to finding systems that work for her clients make her an expert who is easy to learn from. Morgan helps people learn real, effective strategies to face their clutter and organizing challenges head-on. Her book will help many people gain the knowledge they need to take back their home, one step at a time."

—**Michele Vig**, founder of Neat Little Nest and author of *The Holistic Guide to Decluttering*

TAKE BACK YOUR HOME

Other Books by Morgan Tyree

Take Back Your Time (2019)

Your Hospitality Personality (2020)

The Productivity Zone (2023)

TAKE BACK YOUR HOME

How to Organize Every Room for a Stress-Free, Mess-Free, Happy Home

BY MORGAN TYREE

Miami

Copyright © 2025 by Morganize with Me, LLC.
Published by Mango Publishing, a division of Mango Publishing Group, Inc.

Cover Design: Elina Diaz
Cover Photo/illustration: stock.adobe.com/Pixel-Shot
Interior Photographs: Morganize with Me, LLC.
Layout & Design: Elina Diaz

Mango is an active supporter of authors' rights to free speech and artistic expression in their books. The purpose of copyright is to encourage authors to produce exceptional works that enrich our culture and our open society.

Uploading or distributing photos, scans or any content from this book without prior permission is theft of the author's intellectual property. Please honor the author's work as you would your own. Thank you in advance for respecting our author's rights.

For permission requests, please contact the publisher at:
Mango Publishing Group
5966 South Dixie Highway, Suite 300
Miami, FL 33143
info@mango.bz

For special orders, quantity sales, course adoptions and corporate sales, please email the publisher at sales@mango.bz. For trade and wholesale sales, please contact Ingram Publisher Services at customer.service@ingramcontent.com or +1.800.509.4887.

Take Back Your Home: How to Organize Every Room for a Stress-Free, Mess-Free, Happy Home

Library of Congress Cataloging-in-Publication number: 2024946260
ISBN: (print) 978-1-68481-707-8, (ebook) 978-1-68481-708-5
BISAC category code: HOM019000, HOUSE & HOME / Cleaning, Caretaking & Organizing

To my parents, Steve and Janet—
You taught me all I know about home management,
inspired my path to entrepreneurship,
and allowed me to rearrange my room on repeat.

"The purpose of setting goals is to win the game. The purpose of building systems is to continue playing the game. True long-term thinking is goal-less thinking. It's not about any single accomplishment. It is about the cycle of endless refinement and continuous improvement. Ultimately, it is your commitment to the process that will determine your progress."

—James Clear

CONTENTS

Foreword—Cassandra Aarssen · 10

Introduction—Your Home · 12

Part I—Organizing Shapes · 18

Part II—Organizing Snags · 32

Chapter One: Preferences (Ryan) · 37
Chapter Two: Values (Erika) · 50
Chapter Three: Schedules (Shannon) · 58
Chapter Four: Experiences (Bill) · 65
Chapter Five: Purchases (Stacey) · 75
Chapter Six: Memories (Tiffany) · 86
Chapter Seven: Abilities (Debbie) · 96

Part III—Organizing Systems · 106

Chapter Eight: Storing · 118
Chapter Nine: Cooking · 125
Chapter Ten: Living · 141
Chapter Eleven: Bathing · 147
Chapter Twelve: Clothing · 154
Chapter Thirteen: Playing/Working · 161
Chapter Fourteen: Sleeping · 169

Part IV—Organizing Strategies · 174

Conclusion—Your Habits · 184

Acknowledgements · 187

About the Author · 189

Foreword

You are going to be so glad you picked up this book! As a recovering super slob turned organizing expert (TV host, author, and podcaster), I know how overwhelming it can feel to keep an "organized home." I struggled for years with clutter and then learned that I don't organize in the traditional way. This fact—that organizing is not a one-size-fits-all formula—was a game changer for me.

We are all shaped differently, and, when you begin from this position of understanding, you will set yourself up for organizing success! Morgan will teach you how to identify your unique organizing shape style which will help you to understand how and why you organize in the ways that you do. Knowing yourself better is foundational to your organizing journey. Only then can you cull and curate systems in successful ways for YOU.

Not only will you learn how you best organize within your organizing shape, you will discover which snags are getting in your way. You will be challenged to ask yourself some heartfelt questions. For example, which life experiences are holding you back because of past pain points or triggers? Do you find yourself overbuying because you are trying to make up for not having what you wanted or needed as a child? Are you overly prioritizing memories and consequently feeling burdened by the weight of all your keepsakes? Is your schedule overcrowded, and has this resulted in every room in your home also feeling overstuffed? Do your tendencies toward perfectionism keep you stuck in the mode of paralysis by analysis?

Morgan will also teach you how to peel back the layers of what she calls the "organizing onion" to recognize (maybe for the first time ever) what is truly holding you back and how to move forward. You will be able to release the snags and progress forward in a more intentional way. She will, like a trusted friend, gently guide you on how to create effective and long-lasting organizing systems for any space in your home.

If you are really serious about getting from where you are to where you want to be, you need to get to the heart of "why" you are stuck. Then and only then can you turn to the "how-to." Once you get through your snags, you can better organize your spaces. Developing effective organizing systems requires a yin and yang, your heart and your head. If you are ready to conquer your clutter and live your best life, you need the tips, tools, and techniques in *Take Back Your Home.* It will give you every tool you need to take back your home.

Cheers to living clutter-free and organizing within your unique style!

—**Cassandra Aarssen**, blogger and YouTuber behind *ClutterBug* and author of *Cluttered Mess to Organized Success*, *Real Life Organizing*, and others

Introduction
YOUR HOME

"Your home is within your control. It should be the place where you escape all negative forces in the world. Your home should be the antidote to stress, not the cause."

—Peter Walsh

Are you irritated you can't find what you need when you need it? Exhausted from all the stuff that has made its way into your home? When it comes to getting organized, are you overwhelmed with how and where to start?

Well, I have some good news! You are not alone, and you are reading the right book!

Working as a professional organizer for the past decade, this incredible experience has revealed to me the universal challenges we are all trying to navigate when it comes to living more organized, or what I call "morganized." During our initial conversation, many of my clients share that they feel stuck and overwhelmed. They tell me they don't know where to start and are tired of feeling out of control. This is no way to live, yet many of us do, day in and day out. We are stressed by our clutter, drowning in decision fatigue, and overwhelmed by an abundance of stuff. Life is messy and managing our messes is hard. I want to help you live with less mess and stress. Doesn't that sound amazing?

My love for home décor began at a young age. I was born, the oldest of three girls, to a custom homebuilder (my dad) and a designer and seamstress (my mom). My parents modeled to me, almost effortlessly, how to set up an intentional home and the importance of good design. As a child, I would take house plan magazines with me to bed at night and pore over them. I would plan the ins and outs of my future dream home, going room by room, and taking notes of every detail. When I went to apply to college, I considered getting a degree in architecture before finally settling on a degree in business and entrepreneurship.

My love for all things home began at home. Within the four walls of my childhood home, I learned how to keep my spaces within my control, and this eventually led me to coach others on how to do the same. The beauty of my upbringing was the great example my parents provided on how to enjoy and maintain your home. It is important to make space for both. I also learned when you live your life more organized, you live with more peace. And this is what I want to help you experience too.

Deep down we all want our homes to be a place of rest and retreat, yet many of us don't feel or experience this when we are at home. Which is why I want to help you *take back your home.* Your home should be your haven, your sanctuary. The place where you feel *most* at peace. Not the place where you feel like *all* you are doing is trying to pick up the pieces. (Although, to clarify, organizing your home will require some picking up.)

I'm guessing you reached for this book because you feel drained and worn out. You are tired of running on the hamster wheel of disorganization, desperately wanting to get off but not knowing how. Well, these pages will change that for you, once and for all!

Will your home be suddenly magazine-photo-shoot-ready or Pinterest-perfect? Probably not. And frankly, who wants to live in a state of perfection? That's too much to keep up with. I suspect what you need and want, at your core, is a home that meets your needs and functions well for you and for those whom you share your spaces with. In addition, you want to find what you need when you need it. (This is my number one goal with organization.) Organizing doesn't need to be picture-perfect or aesthetically arranged. While this may add to your joy, it's not a requirement to the curation of a tidy home. The purpose of organizing your home is to bring order, because order helps you to minimize your stress, anxiety, and fatigue.

Organizing effectively requires two parts: your heart and your head. Within the organizing process, it is helpful to first emotionally process and prioritize your stuff and then logically implement systems and strategies. When you commit to working first through your layers of hesitation from a heart perspective, you will then be better equipped to tackle your organization in a more healthy and holistic way. This is what we will explore and where we will focus.

You will begin by taking a short quiz for which there are no wrong answers—yay! The quiz will help you identify your specific organizing shape and how you naturally approach organizing within your life. You will glean how to accept your personal organizing style and then how to move through any feelings of hesitation and/or perfectionism. Learning the "why" behind your organizing tendencies will help you feel empowered and equipped to move forward within your style and in the ways that best suit your life.

Next, we will dive into seven common organizing snags (which I also refer to as layers). Is shopping and acquiring stuff your downfall? Are you prone to holding on to everything because of all your cherished memories? Do you tend to do things out of habit even though they aren't aligned with your values? These questions and more will be answered to help you better understand your heart and feelings surrounding your approach to organizing. And guess what? You probably don't need more storage bins, a fancy label maker, or a paper shredder. Although these tools can be helpful, they are usually not the first step to getting organized.

In this section you will learn from my clients and their experiences. Erika will share how hard it was for her to pack up her children's completed Lego sets and box them away in storage. You will learn from Bill about why his struggles with paper organization have more to do with his parents' example of financial management and less to do with his ability to process paper. You will meet Stacey and learn how she fell into a pattern of over-buying and found herself burdened with regret. Their stories will touch your heart and help you know you are not alone on your journey. For the record, we *all* have challenges with organizing and living intentionally. The best course of action is to name your obstacles and then make every effort to push through them.

Then we will turn more practical and hands-on. I will cover seven spaces within the home. You will learn methods to help you transform your spaces. There will be no lessons on how to meticulously fold sheets or arrange books in rainbow order, but instead, realistic systems you can put into place easily and ones that will work for your everyday life. These examples fall within the *good enough* category. Systems that look like baskets, dumping grounds, and hooks. It's Organizing 101, the how-to. An approach that will provide you with the freedom to live with more order. A setup where perfection is not encouraged, but intention most definitely is. And there will be a checklist for each space that you can check off as you tidy up! If that sort of thing motivates you.

In part four, I will explore how to organize strategically. You will learn the tools I have discovered that work within every area of your life to help you live more organized. Themes like boundaries, prioritizing, and scheduling will be the overarching message, because these are the heartbeats behind intentional living. The tools in this section are ones you can begin to apply immediately.

They will help you move into action. We will also touch on neurodivergent conditions that can inhibit your ability to organize. Many of my clients wrestle with ADHD (attention deficit hyperactivity disorder) or other conditions and I see firsthand how much harder it can be to organize when you are navigating feelings of anxiety or have greater difficulty focusing. I will help you learn how to steer your home organization if you (or others) have these condition(s). There will be tips sprinkled throughout the book and an interview in this section with my client Courtney who has an ADHD diagnosis.

If you are ready to move through the barriers of getting started, address your feelings of overwhelm, and finally conquer the obstacles that keep you from implementing and maintaining organizational systems—commit to reading this book *and* applying the tools. And I challenge you to commit! I can't begin to tell you how many dusty books on organizing (good books, I might add) I've unpiled while helping clients sort and edit their belongings. You can't make this stuff up.

It is imperative you make the choice to move from aspiration to action. Learn where to start, what to do, and then most importantly how to keep going. Make a pledge to *take back your home*! Because when you do, and your home feels less chaotic, you will be able to live more fully and more peacefully. And most importantly—find what you need when you need it!

Lastly, this book is meant to be a toolbox. Please feel free to jump around and pick up the tool you most need now. Maybe you already know you struggle with shopping and your habit of over-purchasing is the specific layer you need to peel back. Start with Chapter 5. Or perhaps you are somewhat naturally organized, but you can't seem to get your kitchen under control. Then, skip to Chapter 9, where I break down the basics of how to organize your kitchen or what I refer to as your cooking spaces. Allow these pages to serve and guide you where you need to go the most. There will also be pictures sprinkled throughout the book and my intention in showing you these is to give you "real" life examples. I'm presenting you with a range of homes that have different organizing styles and systems. The common theme is that each of these homes are being lived in well.

Now is the time. We'll get to the heart of getting organized and you will get *more* organized!

Part I
ORGANIZING SHAPES

"TO KNOW THYSELF IS THE BEGINNING OF WISDOM."

—Socrates

I never make my bed. There, I said it. I want to make my bed, but I don't. I know this may come as a surprise to you. People often think that because I'm a professional organizer that everything in my life must be tidied to a "t." Some things are, some of the time, but not *everything* all the time. Life happens. Here's the deal, I don't make my bed because it's not important enough to me and therefore I do not prioritize it as a task. Yes, I've heard that making your bed is the first thing you should do each day, it sets the direction for your day, and gets you off on the right foot. Blah, blah, blah. But for me, it doesn't impact my day in any way—positively or negatively. The reality is I don't spend much time upstairs where my bedroom is and therefore it's an out-of-sight, out-of-mind situation. I share this with you to give you permission to be *you*. To organize your home in the ways that work for you. You have your own organizing style and I want to help you own it! Getting organized can feel challenging and overwhelming. We look at pictures in magazines or on social media and think it's all about sourcing the right products, having a home with ample or well-designed storage, and the always-needed solution of more time. And, while yes, these pieces can be of benefit, they are not the organizing tools we *really* need. First and foremost, what we need is to acknowledge and honor how we are naturally wired. Then, we can get to work on organizing our spaces in the ways that work best for us as individuals.

This begs the question, are we born organized? To which I say, yes and no. Yes, some of us are born with a more detailed or focused nature and others a more creative or relaxed nature. But experiences in life also nurture and guide us along, playing a significant role in how we shape and develop our organizing habits and preferences. The combination of both nature and nurture when woven together within our lives shapes our individual organizing style. Much has gone into your organizational shape and how you approach setting up your home in the ways you do. Often the things we organize or don't organize are because of what was modeled to us. Or we can fall in and out of organizing patterns based on our life circumstances and pressures. Despite all these factors, I believe everyone can organize; however, we all organize differently.

Knowing how to organize begins with *knowing yourself*. When you discover your personal organizing shape, it will become the foundation to helping you get unstuck. Identifying how you see your stuff, how you process your belongings, and how your life exposures have informed your habits, you will then be in a better position to know how and where to start. Begin by pinpointing your organizing shape and you'll be on your way to setting up systems and sorting like a boss! So, what is your organizing shape?

Take this short quiz below and find out.

Your Organizing Shape

Please choose only one answer per question—go with your gut, your first response, the one which sounds the most like you (on most days!).

1. **How would you describe your childhood home?**
   a. structured and formal
   b. comfy and nurturing
   c. loud and boisterous
   d. driven and focused

2. **How do you prefer your bedroom to feel?**
   a. minimal and streamlined
   b. layered and cozy
   c. decorated and colorful
   d. tidy and functional

3. **When you get a text message, how long do you typically take to respond?**
   a. usually less than thirty minutes
   b. within the same day
   c. at most a day or so
   d. in the first five to ten minutes if possible

4. **How do you organize and plan your week?**
   a. keep a detailed calendar and ongoing to-do lists
   b. prefer a visual calendar and pretty lists
   c. plan day by day
   d. use timers, reminders, and a daily schedule

5. **When shopping, what is your general approach?**

   a. I always make a list and keep it with me
   b. I shop as I go and look for sales
   c. I buy things as I need them
   d. I prefer to shop online and schedule deliveries

6. **When it comes to delegating tasks, do you…**

   a. prefer to do things yourself as much as possible
   b. not usually, only if I must or if someone offers
   c. always happy to have someone help
   d. outsource whenever and wherever I can

7. **What do you want others to experience and feel in your home?**

   a. neat and organized
   b. warm and inviting
   c. fun and vibrant
   d. clean and styled

8. **What is your go-to form of entertainment?**

   a. hobbies
   b. quality time with friends and family
   c. socializing and going out
   d. activities and/or entertaining

9. **If you need to select a product or service, what is your typical process?**

   a. take time to research all possible options
   b. ask a friend for a recommendation
   c. use Google or social media
   d. seek referrals and/or check reviews

10. **If you were a shape, which shape would you be?**

    a. diamond
    b. circle
    c. bolt
    d. arrow

11. **Which social setting most fits you?**

    a. Small gathering in a calm environment
    b. Close friends, good conversation, and delicious food
    c. All the people and lots of activity
    d. A special event and/or well-planned gathering

12. **Which best describes the financial foundation in your childhood?**

    a. stability
    b. plenty
    c. wanting
    d. enough

13. **What home design best defines your style?**

    a. Contemporary/Modern
    b. Farmhouse/Craftsman
    c. Bungalow/Cottage
    d. Traditional/Colonial

14. **Which personality type sounds most like you?**

    a. The Thinker
    b. The Supporter
    c. The Socializer
    d. The Director

15. **How far out do you plan a vacation or trip?**

    a. twelve months or more
    b. three to six months out
    c. a month or so
    d. at least six months out

16. **If you set a goal, how do you plan to achieve your goal?**

    a. Create a strategic plan with detailed steps to follow
    b. Make a vision board and ask my friends to join me
    c. Brainstorm and create visuals
    d. Write it out, start planning, and add action items to my schedule

17. Which sport would you most likely want to participate in?

a. running, swimming, or biking
b. walking, yoga, or Pilates
c. dance class, martial arts, or CrossFit
d. golfing, skiing, or tennis

18. How would your friends best describe you?

a. serious, loyal, and thoughtful
b. friendly, kind, and giving
c. entertaining, fun, and energetic
d. leader, detailed, and motivated

19. In your home, which do you prefer the most?

a. Everything tucked away, clean surfaces, and minimal visual clutter
b. Memories sprinkled throughout, soft colors, and a warm sense of welcome
c. Bright colors, eclectic furniture, and items displayed showing my personality
d. A flow and purpose to every space, items in their "homes," and purposeful design

Add up the number of times you answered each number, fill in the total below, and then circle the organizing shape with the highest number (and/or two if there is a tie).

Total number (A) _____ Diamond

Total number (B) _____ Circle

Total number (C) _____ Bolt

Total number (D) _____ Arrow

This quiz helps you define how you tend to organize within the different facets of your life. It is likely you found yourself closely between two shapes and that is more than okay! Often, we may organize differently at home than we may at the office or vice versa. We also can have different prioritization with how we organize within the different areas of our lives (schedules, commitments, stuff), which may also affect scoring similarly between two or more shapes. Most importantly, notice what your shape(s) says about you and then what this means with how you set up your organizational systems and strategies. Let's dive deeper into each one.

Arrows

Organizing isn't all that challenging for you because you have a clear direction for every area of your life. You are decisive, scheduled, and always ready to delegate your tasks to others. Your spaces are generally neat and tidy, and you also appreciate pleasing decor and intentional design. Being goal-focused and using good prioritization helps you to achieve big results. You appreciate an organized space and are generally good at taking care of the required daily and weekly tasks that help you keep your systems intact. You fall somewhat naturally into the "born organized" category and are also a fan of outsourcing things to help you stretch your time. When you get stuck with organizing it is often tied to a specific preference you might be holding on to, an important value you want to protect, or your desire to keep meaningful traditions alive. You will discover how to push through these tendencies and let some of these things go when and where applicable.

Bolts

When it comes to organizing, it's likely this is not a high priority for you. It's one of those "to-dos" that sounds nice, but if you are honest, you would rather spend time doing almost anything else! You aspire to be organized because it seems like a good idea; however, your time and energy are usually spent in more creative, relaxed ways. You prefer your belongings to be on display in colorful ways. Your spaces represent all parts of your life in the most memorable ways. Selective organizing is likely what you do most of the time. This means, you only organize the items and categories that matter the most to you; we all do this in one form or another and it is encouraged! Your organizing snags are likely with memorabilia, shopping and acquiring, and the various life experiences that have formed you. We will unpack these patterns and you'll learn how to dial up your level of organizing to then help you pursue even more of your passions!

Circles

Aesthetics and design rank highly for you in all areas of your life. You have a peaceful, easygoing, and Zen-like demeanor. Decorating and styling in your life look like colors, patterns, and textures. You like to organize, but you can get overly focused on presentation which then can lead to missing the function you were aiming for in the first place. Some areas of your life are organized, but many areas also fall into a more relaxed, go-with-the-flow mode of operation. Your home represents your life story with beautiful creative expressions sprinkled throughout. What gets in your way of getting organized are commitments, memories of the past, and those traditions you cherish and want to hold on to. Your softness and thoughtfulness are incredible gifts. And the reality is that you *can* be organized while also keeping things comfortable and manageable. I'll show you how to use your strengths to further develop your organizing habits.

Diamonds

If you had a life motto, it might be, *"A place for everything and everything in its place."* You've yet to meet a spreadsheet that doesn't call your name. You prefer to have things tucked away and clear surfaces are always your preference. Analyzing is your mode of operation. Your desire is for things to be detailed, coordinated, and categorized clearly. Specifics are your jam through and through. Organizing is important to you in all parts of your life. It's common for others to look to you to handle the details in situations because you never miss them, even the smallest ones! While you organize somewhat naturally, you can get stuck in the common trap of paralysis by analysis. Your snags within how you organize tend to be mostly with your preferences, habits, and values. Which we'll get to more!

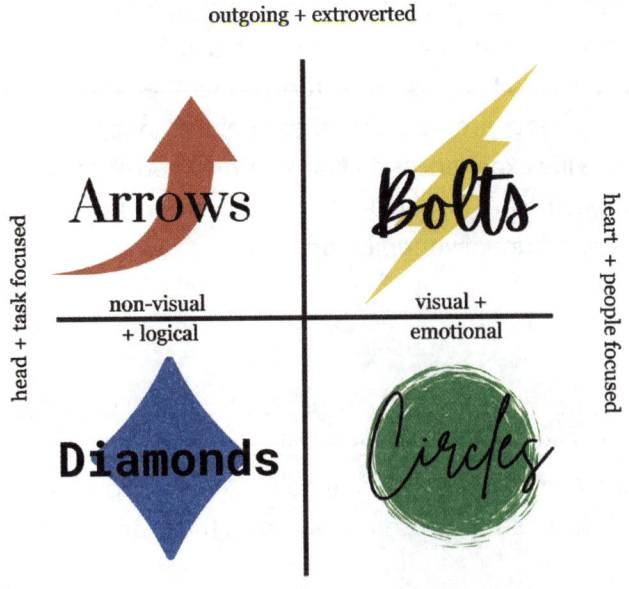

When you know how you are shaped and how you naturally organize, it will help you to make more informed decisions with setting up your organizational systems. For example, if you are an Arrow or Diamond, you probably prefer things in your home to be tucked away. Whereas, if you identified as a Bolt or Circle, you are likely okay with leaving things in your line of sight and prefer to do so. Honor your preferences. Your organizing shape is perfect for *you*. It is your guide, so let it shine the way!

Know Yourself

Many of my clients start working with me on a singular project and then as we move along their project list often grows into additional tasks and spaces. Which means I get the privilege of continuing to service them. This aspect of my business has become one of the best parts of my experience. I love connecting deeper with my clients and becoming what I consider to be friends. We share increased time together and in spending so much time together, I am welcomed into their messes and stresses and get the amazing role of cheering them on. It's a dream job (minus all the mess, ha!). I also want to share that my business is focused on relationships. I work to connect with my clients and understand them. It is a uniqueness to my business model, and I wouldn't have it any other way. In fact, it's my favorite part of my work.

In the beginning of each client relationship, I work to identify my client's organizing shape. This helps me to better know how they think through projects and what importance they place on their belongings. When I know how they tend to approach organizing, I can guide them more intentionally through the organizational process. I don't come in with a cookie-cutter approach on how to organize their spaces. Instead, I listen intently and let them lead me down their organizing path. I'm there as a professional and accountability partner. I'm not there to make them organize like me or someone else.

I encourage you to *know yourself*. When you better understand what's important to you and your natural tendencies, it will help you establish what you want to prioritize organizing. Embrace yourself and your uniqueness. Don't be too hard on yourself. Organizing can be fun! What often gets in the way is our inclination to compare or look outward for direction and inspiration. Yes, there are great resources out there, but nobody knows you like you do! Be confident with how you want to set up your spaces. Choose to be content with organizing the areas that matter the most to *you*.

> **Knowing how to organize begins with *knowing yourself*.**

Take some time to consider your organizing shape(s) and what they mean to you. Contemplate what's working for you and what might need some gentle adjusting. We are all a work in progress, and I want to help you to continue taking steps forward.

Next, we will explore the different snags that impact your ability to get organized. We are going to peel back the organizing onion to help you better understand which hindrances may be blocking your progress. Even more importantly, you will learn how to successfully move through them. If you have a pair of kitchen goggles—the ones designed to help you not cry while you peel onions—go put them on! I'm kidding. Well, maybe not.

Part II
ORGANIZING SNAGS

"WHATEVER WE FACE, WE HAVE A CHOICE: WILL WE BE BLOCKED BY OBSTACLES, OR WILL WE ADVANCE THROUGH AND OVER THEM?"

—Ryan Holiday

When I started my professional organizing business, I assumed most of my clients would be homeowners used to outsourcing many of their home-related tasks and would therefore be more likely to prioritize a luxury service like in-home organizing. And while this is true for some of my clients, it is not the majority. I have worked with all types of clients. I had a client who enlisted my services at her gorgeous second home in Aspen, Colorado, and another, a parent, who hired me to help unpack and organize his disorganized college student. The need for in-home organizing help is deep and wide. We all have stuff to manage and maintain. We all have obstacles that get in our way and it's easy to fall and not know how to get back up. Every one of us has what I call an "organizing onion," and each layer needs to be peeled back. Hitting a snag when trying to get organized can feel defeating.

When we lived overseas in Portugal, I discovered my love for Indian food. We frequented a restaurant and I always looked forward to their tasty meals. I loved the combination of spices and flavors and became a major fan of curry dishes. A major ingredient in Indian food is onions. I say this to remind you that onions, when peeled, taste great (to most). However, unpeeled onions serve little to no purpose. If you desire to live more purposefully, commit to getting to your core. The organizing onion is what I consider to be your stumbling block. It represents those things deep within you, keeping you stuck with getting organized. If you desire to live intentionally and set up your home in organized ways, the organizing onion must be acknowledged.

However, we often don't want to peel back the layers and examine our thoughts and feelings because it is emotional work. Trust me, I know this firsthand. I'd rather keep on moving and check off my to-do list than take the time and energy to ask myself hard questions. It can be difficult to take a closer look at ourselves and analyze why we do things the way we do. It takes effort, and it can sometimes be harder than the work we desire to do (which, in this case, is getting organized). But if we don't start peeling back the layers and naming our obstacles, we will continue to zig-zag through our organizing tasks and find ourselves unable to cross the finish line with our projects. You picked up this book because you're exhausted and frustrated, and you don't want to stay stuck. So, pick up your peeler!

The layers you need to expose can range from ingrained habits to values you hold close to commitments you've made. At the core of the organizing

Part II: Organizing Snags

onion is recognizing that how you do something often has an even deeper invisible reason, which then reveals itself visibly. Your external physical clutter is usually because you are overloaded internally with your mental clutter. This is why you must first look on the inside before focusing on the outside. Read through the seven organizing snags and identify which ones speak to your heart. Some of them may resonate with you; others may not. Your objective will be to name what you are stumbling on. Which layers are showing up in your life and then consider how your organizing shape also plays a role.

> **Your external physical clutter is usually because you are overloaded internally with your mental clutter.**

Are you super sentimental with items and memories, and is this impeding your decluttering progress? Do you find yourself falling into a pattern of mindless shopping because if you are honest, you like the nice release of dopamine it provides? What were some unhealthy examples modeled to you in your childhood that you may have taken on without even realizing? Does your home and life reflect what you say you value? Are you trying to navigate organizing but struggle with either ADHD or OCD, or maybe both?

There are often tears when we dig into the "why" behind the issues that keep us from enjoying our best life. But tears help us to heal and enable us to move forward. This process will require dedication, but you are worth it. If you desire more calmness and less chaos, you must get to your core. When you address the hindrances in your way you will feel less overwhelmed and better equipped to move from *aspiration to action.* Let's get ready to peel and analyze. It will sting, but it will be worth it. And as I mentioned in the introduction chapter, please feel free to skip to any chapter that speaks to you immediately. It is likely some of these examples are challenges for you and others are not. Use these pages as a manual and toolbox. Keep it simple and examine only what is meaningful to you and your process.

Which obstacles are impeding you from getting started in the first place? Why are they causing you to stumble? What can you do to overcome the snags? Consider these questions as I introduce you to my precious clients—special individuals who have touched my life more deeply than I could ever touch theirs.

Chapter One

Preferences

"Simple can be harder than complex: You have to work hard to get your thinking clean to make it simple. But it's worth it in the end because once you get there, you can move mountains."

—Steve Jobs

One summer, my client Ryan had reached out to me saying he needed help with his paper organization. As a busy owner of multiple construction businesses, he was drowning amidst his paperwork. I was excited to learn he needed help with his office organization because I spend a lot of my time in dusty basements and crowded garages. So, the thought of wearing a business-casual outfit and working in a downtown loft office sounded delightful!

At our first meeting he pulled up to his office, his truck filled to the brim with boxes and piles of paper. I casually said, "It doesn't look like that much work." Little did I know what was ahead of us and I also started regretting I had worn wedge shoes. We hauled the boxes and piles up a full flight of stairs to his office and stacked everything on the ping-pong table which also doubled as a conference room table. It took us quite some time to work through the many stacks of paper. Over the course of several months, we sorted and processed every piece of paper within one to two scheduled organizing sessions per week. The challenges were the sheer quantity of paper and that all his business and personal papers were commingled. After spending a significant amount of time working to get things organized, I'm happy to report that by late that fall his papers were all organized and put away. We created a file cabinet for current-year documents, dedicated past-year papers to long-term file boxes, and set up a daily in-and-out mailbox system. It felt so good to get the chaos under control!

Here is the paperwork we had to wade through, partially organized on the ping pong table in his office.

Ryan is extremely detailed and all about consistency and accuracy. The first time these traits were highlighted to me was when he specified, he would like his receipts filed and organized by the exact time of purchase (not just month or day) in ascending order. His preferences were clear. Crystal clear. While this didn't seem important to me, it was important to him. And while I always want to steer my clients toward efficiency, I also want to respect their inclinations and help them organize in the ways that work best for them. It's important to honor specific tastes, and I encourage you to do this for yourself too.

Everything all organized and filed away.

His close attention to detail and desire for things to be *just right* is why it was easy for me to ask him to pick out new paint colors for my house (and he also happens to own a painting business). Because he gives so much thought to every decision he makes, I knew he would give careful consideration and spend more attention choosing paint selections than I ever would. While I like color and design, I can also feel overwhelmed when I must make such a permanent decision. A decision that is likely to be on full display for a decade, if not more!

Well, he did not disappoint. Ryan arrived at my house with around thirty quarts of sample paint colors. My husband, David, and I asked him which colors he thought would go well together and he picked out a great combination of four colors and set them in front of us. It was a unanimous vote for both me and David. We didn't need to think about it, nor did we need to see more options. We trusted his expertise. I think Ryan was surprised we didn't require more time to think things over and we were so clear on our choice. But we were—we were crystal clear.

We all have preferences in how we do things, and this shows up for each of us in our homes. We tend to set things up in the ways that work for us and in how we prefer things to look and feel. And while it's important to honor your preferences, it is equally important to realize when and where some of your preferences might be diminishing your productivity and/or progress. I continue to work with Ryan, and we are always working toward increasing his efficiency, while also allowing for his preferences.

All of us need to align our preferences to our desired progress within our organizing tasks. One way to do this is by being strategic with what you macro and micro sort. Another way is to identify when you should be fixed with a certain setup and where you could benefit from more flexibility. And when it comes to aesthetics, it can look nice to have things neatly arranged and coordinated, but it is not the end-all, be-all. Let me explain.

Macro/Micro

When it comes to organizing, I generally recommend starting with a macro approach. This means beginning with a grand-scheme strategy. It looks like corralling all your paper together, piling your clothes in one spot, or grouping your like items together—toys, kitchen appliances, cleaning products. Getting things "like with like" will help you see how many items you have within each category. When you can visually see a full category of your grouped items it will then make it easier for you to process what stays and what goes. Once you have your like items in macro piles, then you go micro and start to edit.

For example, if you pull your thirty-nine pairs of shoes together and set them all out on the floor, you will then have a better lens to help you decide how many pairs of shoes you want to keep and which ones you want to donate or sell. You will see how many styles are similar, how many pairs are worn out, and how many of them you've never worn. Raise your hand if you are guilty. Me too.

Beginning with a macro approach is an easier starting point. It's simple. All you need to do is create groups. Always start macro. If you have camping supplies (and you actually go camping), then all the supplies you use for camping should be stored together. This will give you a great starting place and it won't require much decision-making. In fact, for many categories you may not need to go much further than macro sorting. If your camping supplies all fit in a few bins and the storage and organization works well for you, then you have a system! You don't need to take any further steps.

Don't overcomplicate things; this is often why we don't finish an organizing task. We think we need to hyper-sort and overthink everything, but we don't. If you resonate with the tendency to overthink and this keeps you vacillating over how to do things, stay with a macro approach whenever and wherever you can. Macro systems look like putting all your smoothie ingredients on one shelf, placing all gift-wrapping supplies together in a cupboard, or designating a shoe basket by the front door, for shoes! Keep things macro where you can, and you'll keep things simple. Simple systems work.

While you may prefer to micro-sort things or go deeper with your level of organization, because it can look prettier, keep in mind that micro sorting does not create a better system. In fact, it can often require even more upkeep and who needs more to do? Only go micro when there is an added benefit to you and if you can maintain it. An illustration of this could be your closet. A macro setup of your clothes could look like short-sleeved shirts together and long-sleeved shirts together, and this could be enough. Maybe you blend sleeveless within the short sleeves and three-quarter-length sleeves in with the long sleeves. You don't need to micro-sort further and colorize every shirt within those two categories or go in order from sleeveless to long sleeve. But, if those steps are important to you, *and* you will keep up with the colorizing and micro sorting, then by all means do so. However, it is not a requirement to curate an organized closet. You get to define what an organized closet looks like to you. The goal of organization is to find things; if you can find your shirts easily then your system works.

Now there are certain categories where micro sorting is necessary. For instance, if you are working to organize papers with important information, then once you have all your papers combined you will need to do a detailed micro sort. Micro sorting is required for items that hold a higher value of importance, have a requirement for record-keeping, and/or need more attention in general. Paper is a good example because it touches all three of these requirements. Realize though that when you need to micro-sort things, it will be more time-consuming and mentally draining. It tends to require greater focus and attention. Choose to only micro-organize those areas which are the most important to you or require you to do so. Otherwise go macro with your organizing anywhere you can!

Fixed/Flexible

It's easy to become rigid when you want to organize a space. You can fall into thinking you must find the exact style of bins or set of beautiful matching hangers, or if you just had more space, *then* you could get everything organized. While it can be helpful to have these pieces in place, keep in mind that within the organizing puzzle you can still get organized even if you don't have all the right pieces. It's more about using the pieces you have and using them well. There is a place for rigidity within organizing. For example, yes, keep your tax receipts for the seven years, but you may not need to keep copies of your paid utility statements for a home you lived in fifteen years ago (and have since sold). There is a sweet spot within organizing. There is a happy medium where you can experience the benefits of organization without having to spend all your time organizing. Organization is meant to be life-giving, not life-taking!

If you have more of a fixed mindset, evaluate where you can loosen up. I would recommend striving for a mindset of *good enough*. If you overanalyze things, adjust your thinking to broader sections and divisions. Your time and energy can easily be spent trying to perfect things and this can work in the opposite direction. Often Arrows and Diamonds will wrestle more with these tendencies. Avoid the habit of spending too much time thinking about the process instead of processing what needs to be processed. (Say that three times fast!) Avoid getting stuck in this predicament. The desire for perfection can delay your progress and the momentum you want to achieve.

> **I would recommend striving for a mindset of *good enough*.**

Where do you think you land? Are you more of a fixed thinker or a flexible thinker? Realizing where you hover is important to identify and then make a point to adjust your thinking up or down where needed. This can be beneficial. Because when you are too far on either end of the spectrum, your feelings of overwhelm will get in your way. Being consumed by your thoughts can limit your ability to move forward. In the same way, if you are in the habit of being overly flexible with everything and your home and life show for it, consider where you should tighten the reins. An emphasis on *good enough* is a great sounding board. You can also find freedom by designating some areas as fixed and some as flexible. Allow yourself to relax in the spaces you can, and you'll free up your time and energy. And give yourself permission to have fixed systems in spaces where you will benefit from greater detail and order. There are places and spaces for both. Circles and Bolts, you are naturally good at staying relaxed so keep this up!

A good system is intuitive. I like to give the example of a kindergarten classroom. If you walk into the classroom, you will probably see where to hang your coat, where to put your lunchbox, and where the markers are located. Things are usually clearly labeled and sorted; it's hyper-obvious where things belong.

Remember, there is no perfect system! You simply need a system that works for you. Find a happy medium between fixed and flexible and you'll be well on your way.

Aesthetic/Non-aesthetic

There is a trend on social media where creators are showing their lived-in, non-aesthetic homes. I love this! Because while social media (or any form of media) can provide us with inspiration, it can equally be a great source of frustration. Which is why this trend is so awesome! The homeowners are making their normal homes normal. It's refreshing and encouraging. They are spreading the message that yes, you can have an outdated home and it can still function and work well for your family. In fact, that lived-in look and those messy signs of life often contribute to an increasingly comfy home. I love seeing the outdated kitchen cabinets and unfashionable lighting, because none of these details set the tone for an organized or disorganized home. What sets the tone is you and how you use your spaces.

While we know it's *not* necessary to have everything new, shiny, and harmonious, this is the example we mostly see. We are inundated with stunning pictures of gorgeous, stocked pantries, tidied playrooms, and cohesive bedrooms (and usually no signs of "living"). So, let's ask some questions. How aesthetically minded are you? Do you need to simmer a bit in this area to help you with your organizing progress? Or could some additional layering and styling help you in your home to create more cohesiveness?

I use the term *aesthetically aware* with my clients to help determine how important aesthetics are to them and how they want to organize their spaces. Some clients want everything to match, and others don't care at all about this piece. I don't believe it is necessary to spend money on organizing products to make everything match. Yes, sometimes this is helpful, but what's even more helpful and costs less, is to start by using what you already own. While I prefer things to look good aesthetically, I also make a point to give myself permission to keep things simpler so I can get the job done. If over-coordinating things or hyper-focusing on details is slowing my progress, I will choose a simpler path.

Matching bins like these from The Container Store can add increased function as they stack better and will help you to maximize space.

A good rule of thumb is to name your non-negotiables. Is it essential to you that all your hangers match? Would you prefer to get new storage bins in the same color and style, so they stack better and fill your space more fully? Tired of having dishes that don't fit in your cupboard and you know getting new dishes would make an impact? Choose to make changes in the areas where the adjustments will change the game. But likewise, also decide what can be left alone. If your file folders don't match, but they are all labeled and organized, let them be. If something isn't broken, don't spend time and energy trying to fix it. If cramming your receipts for the year into one folder (in any order whatsoever) works well enough for you then that's your system. Another filter I also consider is how often I will see something or need to retrieve it. If an item falls into a tucked away or out-of-sight spot, I will spend less energy on the aesthetics. I would rather save that energy for the visual and more prominent places in my home. This way every time I see the aesthetics I can appreciate the level of detail I put in.

Knowing your tastes will allow you to better orchestrate systems and strategies that will work well for you and for the long term. Preferences can either be a launch pad or a limitation. I encourage you to take a step back and see which of your preferences may be standing in your way and then allow yourself to adjust. Deliberate and gentle adjustments surrounding your preferences can be the catalyst you need to get unstuck and more organized!

Takeaways to Take Back Your Home

- Considering your organizing shape, what strengths of your style help you prioritize organizing? And likewise, what weaknesses in your organizing shape are inhibiting your progress?

- Think about the big picture and list what you desire from your home. How do you want your spaces to serve you and others? Then identify which preferences are potentially negatively impacting your abilities to get organized and/or set up your spaces as you would like them to look and feel.

- What is one space you need to macro sort? Or which categories and/or spaces are you micro-sorting items where you could relax more and keep things more macro?

Chapter Two

Values

"It's not hard to make decisions when you know what your values are."

—Roy Disney

As a parent of three, I have struggled to maneuver through the changing seasons my kids are experiencing. It seems as soon as I get one phase under control (loosely, I might add), my kids have already moved into their next phase. It can be as big of a change as shifting from being their carpool driver to their copilot/driving instructor. Or as small as when they announce they no longer like the granola bars they used to eat every day. (The same granola bars I just bought three cases of at Costco!) With each new chapter comes different sizes, preferences, and desires. Kids grow fast and so do their ever-changing needs. I have also realized I was more organized BK (before kids). As we have grown our family, our belongings have also exponentially expanded! I find myself the orchestrator of all this added stuff and some days it exhausts me. It was so much easier to stay on top of stuff when it was just *my* stuff.

When my client Erika and I first talked, she opened her heart to me and expressed how she was grieving the changing of seasons with her kids. Her children were growing up and moving on to different interests and activities. When speaking about the changes, Erika began to tear up. It was touching and I could relate all too easily as we had just sent our second child off to college. Parenting and raising kids require a lot of time and energy. Erika needed to do a big sort and purge of childhood toys and wanted someone to help her navigate through the feelings and process. She wanted help reclaiming her time, energy, and the spaces in her home.

I'll never forget when she shared with me during an organizing session, *"We live hard."* Their family valued seizing life to the fullest. This was highlighted by the fact that they had built a basketball court in their backyard. They prioritized their kids and wanted their home to be a place full of fun and activity. A space where basketball games with friends was encouraged. However, the memories of raising a family with the mantra of living hard were impacting Erika's ability to sort through all the stuff. She had a difficult time separating the memories from the things that played an important role in creating the memories. It was challenging for her to allow one chapter to end and make room for the next.

We can value many things, and I will touch on three types that can impact your home organization: personal, home, and social. Exploring each of these will help you better pinpoint the hurdles you may be facing and how you can successfully get over them.

Personal Values

One of Erika's goals was to pack the completed Lego sets that lined her dining room on side tables and store them elsewhere. These Lego sets come with a manual on how to build an intended design. These are detailed projects and her kids had spent hours putting together the intricate sets. Erika had even added extra tables to the room to help display the completed kits. It was beautiful to see, and I love how she made the room focused on her kids. Her values are clearly love and support for her children.

However, now that they were moving into a new season and her kids were no longer regularly playing with Legos, she desired to take back her dining room. The process itself was relatively easy as we were just putting the completed masterpieces into bins that would be moved and stored in the garage. Yet, for Erika, the part that wasn't so easy was experiencing the emotions around the memories of the Legos. She got emotional again as we worked on the project because she was acknowledging that a precious chapter of her life was ending. Erika had placed a high value on being a mom and helping her family *live hard*. Packing up the memories and the recognition was both difficult and bittersweet. Her value wasn't shifting, but her setups, systems, and spaces were.

When it comes to what you value, it can be tough to navigate and reflect on your choices. I want to encourage you to examine your values and let them be the filter for your decisions. Your personal values are anything important to you or what you want to prioritize in your life. They are personal and specific to you. Often family members and friends can impose their values and expectations on you and expect you to value what they do too. Notice what pressures may be impacting you and work to name *your* values and build your life on those values. When you better define what you value, you can then better prioritize your time, energy, and how you spend it.

This is a picture of Erika's craft and school supply area after we reorganized it. Using an armoire is a great option to maximize storage and create a dedicated zone for like items.

Home Values

Just because a room is designed to be an office or a living room doesn't mean you have to set up the room in that way. When it comes to your home, it can be life-giving to reestablish your rooms to best fit your wants and needs. It can be easy to fall into the pattern that we must follow the floor plan as it is. However, we don't! It's your home and you get to define how you want your rooms and spaces to serve you. Start by defining what you need from your home.

If you work from home, then a dedicated home office will be of value. If you have young kids, then a playroom might be beneficial to help corral all the toys in one spot. Or if you don't eat around the table every night for dinner, then perhaps you could redesign the use of your dining room. Consider what you value in your home and then set up room and spaces accordingly.

The only rule is there are no rules! You get to make the rules work for you. What do you value? Take a moment and write two or three values for your home. It is important to this process. My all-important message is *value what you have and have what you value.* Every home has a certain amount of real estate and I encourage you to value the space within your real estate. If you have a stack of dusty boxes piled in a dark corner of your basement and haven't touched them in over ten years, I'm not convinced you value what is in those boxes. While it may not be affecting your day-to-day, it is taking up space and adding to your mental clutter. Your goal should be to prioritize every space in your home and then only put things you use or value within those spaces. And yes, there will be items you don't necessarily value, maybe items like toilet paper or garbage sacks, but I assume they provide you with some value!

Getting organized is usually not about having more space or better storage. Yes, sometimes these pieces can be helpful, but if you start from a position of valuing your home as it is and setting up your home with what you value, then you will make the spaces you have work for your lifestyle. Less is more. Adopt this mindset and become ruthless with what you keep in your home. When you apply this mantra as a value, your things and spaces will serve you better.

My client Kendra reworked her entryway and added this great mudroom/command center to help provide more storage and systems for her family.

Social Values

We have all struggled with trying to "keep up with the Joneses." The term came from a comic strip created over a century ago. *"The strip depicts the social climbing McGinis family, who struggle to 'keep up' with their neighbors, the Joneses of the title. The Joneses were unseen characters throughout the strip's run, often spoken of but never shown."* [1] I find it interesting that the Joneses were never shown in the comic strip and that this idiom is still used to this day. It shows how much we look outside of ourselves for examples of what we should value. And while these days we still have the face-to-face influence, we also have the added pressures of social media.

Either way, the comparison game is a trap. I'm referring specifically to when we see what others have and want what they have too. It is a challenge that has always existed, but in our consumer-driven society it is easier than ever to charge or finance things we don't need or can't afford. The reality is we take notice of what our friends have and buy. From clothes to trips, and to how their homes look. It takes discipline not to be enticed by all the material offerings in our world and at our fingertips. If you struggle with comparison or wanting what others have, I want you to take a step back and look at this from a different perspective. When do you find yourself wrestling with these feelings the most? What do you tend to want more of? Where in your life are you settling and/or doing things for others before yourself?

Go back to what you just named as your personal and home values and use these as your guidelines. If the things you are attracted to don't align with what you said are your personal and home values, then adjust. When you stay focused on what you want to focus on, that's when you'll see the results you are after. Name it and claim it!

To reorganize a space, avoid the time thief of getting on social media searching for ideas. While yes, there are *lots* of great tools and tutorials out there, try instead to set aside a block of time and start to do the work. This will look like macro sorting, then micro sorting. Getting rid of items (selling, donating, recycling), and moving things to their designated spots (remember like with like). And if you don't have permanent spaces (or "homes") yet, work to put everything in categories. Then when you have a bigger system in place you will only need to shift things to their assigned homes. After you've done this foundational work, then you can hop on social media to look for inspiration. Avoid scrolling for forty-five minutes with little to no result to show for it. Value your time and make yourself first do the organizing process.

---

1 Keeping Up with the Joneses, Wikipedia, April 1, 2024, en.wikipedia.org/wiki/Keeping_up_with_the_Joneses#:~:text=The%20phrase%20originates%20with%20the,the%20Joneses%20of%20the%20title.

Value what you have and have what you value.

Erika stayed the course, worked through her emotions, and we got her dining room back to looking like a dining room. We sorted through boxes of toys and did a full assessment. She valued the antique toy trucks that had been her husband's as a child and her children had also played with. Erika wanted to keep those for future grandkids so one day she could hopefully see the memories relived. She also held on to some of the most memorable toys and willingly parted with the ones they no longer needed. She chose well and she and her family continue to *live hard*. The season has changed but Erika's values are realized and remain the driver for her decisions.

Takeaways to Take Back Your Home

- What values have others placed on you that you don't necessarily hold in the same esteem? Which values can you choose not to hold for yourself and/or redefine for you and your home? (If you are shaped as a Bolt or Circle, you may struggle more with being pressured by others.)

- How do you want your home to look and feel? What values do you want to instill in those you share your home with and to guests you welcome in?

- Where could you use some additional boundaries with your social media influence? Do you desire to move toward greater application? How will you do this? What measures can you take?

Chapter Three
Schedules

"The key is in not spending time, but in investing it."

—Stephen R. Covey

My friend Shannon and I met through a Mastermind group for speakers and writers. We spent a year together on Zoom coaching calls and then later had the privilege of meeting face-to-face at the group's retreat in the Pacific Northwest. A couple of years later, I was flattered when she reached out to me for organizing help and even more excited to learn she wanted to fly me out to Michigan to help her unpack from her move. She and her family had recently relocated from Flint to Ann Arbor, Michigan, and were drowning in their moving boxes. So of course, I enthusiastically said, "Yes!" I looked forward to the opportunity to help them settle into their new home.

Shannon shared with me that she felt overwhelmed and desired my expertise to help her with the transition. She wanted to set up her new home in a thoughtful and intentional way. Her goal was to establish effective systems in their home and teach her daughter how to organize and maintain her spaces too. She went on to explain that with her new job and responsibilities, she had less time and energy to take care of everything around the house. I admire Shannon because she was aware of her capacity and capabilities. She didn't have the margin to handle all the details surrounding a full house unpack, not to mention getting things organized. She also acknowledged because they had lived in their previous home for so many years, that they had acquired a lot of belongings. Additional seasons of life and staying in one place usually bring in more layers of stuff.

Over a long weekend in October, I traveled to Michigan to help Shannon and her family get organized and settled in. We spent three full days unpacking, sorting, decluttering, and working to set up effective systems. We took a trip to The Container Store which helped us design a much-needed system in her pantry. We had a heart-to-heart about her clothing inventory and the amount of beauty products. (She agreed to be more thoughtful with her shopping and acquiring.) And we set up her daughter's room, creating zones for everything in the room to help her see everything and know where things should be put away.

Moving is one of the best forms of organizing self-help. When you must touch every single item that you own, it can be incredibly eye-opening. Everyone should have to experience relocation. I have joked there should be a criterion that everyone moves at a minimum of every five to seven years. While this wouldn't solve all our disorganization issues or propensity to acquire, it would help us to be more aware of how much we are accumulating.

After considering your values, I want you to take an inventory of what you are committed to. Investigate if your calendar matches your values. Also ask, what are you physically, emotionally, and mentally *able* to keep up with? Your calendar reveals what you are committed to. Take an honest inventory of your commitments and schedule. Are your energies and efforts being spent in a field you are passionate about? Do you feel you are using your talents and gifts to your fullest? When you finish your day, are you pleased with your accomplishments, or do you dread starting again tomorrow? While not every decision or commitment is fully up to you, many of them *are* up to you. This is what you must explore and evaluate.

> **Your calendar reveals what you are committed to.**

Decide

If there is one thing I've learned, it's that our time is precious. I recently walked through a medical diagnosis with my husband and while his prognosis was good, it still rocked our world. It made my husband and I question everything. I share this to encourage you to keep the big picture in mind for what you want out of your life. Maintain a long-term view while also focusing on your smaller and daily decisions. All your choices work together to make up your life. Choices may range from how much you work, to what career path you choose, to the relationships you protect, to how and where you want to live. The list goes on and on. Commit to carefully and intentionally examining your decisions and using your values to help direct your decision-making.

Every decision has an effect. If I choose to stay up later than my normal bedtime, this choice will likely affect my ability to get up at my normal time the next morning. This might also mean I sacrifice priorities within my morning routine. While this decision may not have much of a short-term effect, making this choice over and over may keep me from achieving bigger goals or outcomes that I say are important.

Consider the ripple effect of every choice you make. If you want to be more organized, you must decide your non-negotiables or risk your negotiables defining you. These are personal filters you must identify and use as a guide. Remember not everything can be done at once. When we try to do too much at one time, that's when our ability to juggle all the balls in the air fails. The better you can get at fine-tuning your highest priorities, the more easily you can manage your home. When you define and decide what to focus on, you can focus more clearly. We all have schedules that pull us in many different directions; however, when we clearly define our priorities, it will help us to better map out our days.

Design

After clearly articulating what you want and/or need to keep on your to-do list, work to design systems that will help you complete your obligations within your related commitments. For example, if you work from home and have a set number of hours you need to log each day, then set up strategies to protect and prioritize your work. It will benefit you to have a designated workspace that minimizes distractions. You will want to communicate with your housemates about your work hours and how they should or should not communicate with you during your work time. Simply saying you need to get work done is not a strategy. However, setting up systems and creating standard operating procedures will help you get started each day and keep moving. A well-designed plan can work wonders. Try it! This can be applied to any household duty, work responsibility, or personal goal. Design a step-by-step plan and then work the plan. This will keep you on track with fulfilling your priorities and honoring your values.

A simple system I would recommend is food prepping. All of us have full lives and the one thing that remains is that we must eat every single day. It's a lot of work to keep up with the weekly food planning, shopping, prepping, and cleaning. Try to block off some time each week to do meal prep. My husband does this with his daily smoothies. Instead of taking all the ingredients out every day, he does it once a week and puts everything into mason jars with lids. They stack neatly, and each morning, all he must do is dump it in the blender, add liquid, and mix it. It's as easy as 1, 2, 3! He found a simple design that helps him save time and ensures he gets his day off on the right track with his nutritious smoothie.

David's smoothies prepped and lined up for the week ahead.

Delegate

If you are shaped as a Diamond or an Arrow, you likely have developed the skill of delegation. But for some delegating to others doesn't come as naturally. Delegation is an art and strong leaders know how to delegate well and it is what makes them effective. This is what Shannon did. She knew she had a big role with her new job, and she also needed to be available to her daughter and husband as they established their new lives in Ann Arbor. She needed to commit to getting moved in, but she wasn't sure how to design the steps and orchestrate the pieces to make it happen. Therefore, she asked for help. She called on someone who does this work regularly and has become an expert. Shannon made the wise decision to do what she could do independently and then delegated the rest.

Parents, I'm talking to you directly right now. If you have kids and they can operate tablets and smartphones, I want to remind you that they can also operate dishwashers and washing machines. Yes, every task should be age-appropriate, but there is no reason a twelve-year-old cannot be doing their laundry or a nine-year-old can't be doing the dishes after dinner. If you feel like keeping up with your housework is too big of a commitment, look for ways to outsource. This can begin with your family members or roommates. Outsourcing is an excellent time management tool and if you are working to become an intentional shopper then I challenge you to take some of that savings from items not needed and put it toward an outsourcing budget. What if you could hire someone to do a deep cleaning of your home once a month? Or hire a landscaper to mow your lawn? Or pay for a meal delivery service to help you save time in the evenings? If you trade consumption of things for budgeting for services, you will likely feel an immediate benefit. You will save time and energy and your home will run more efficiently.

I am not suggesting you outsource everything or that this is the easy way out. I am recommending that if you want to organize and run your home well, it is an option that should be explored. It is important to recognize what you can keep up with and then choose to either delegate those things you can't manage or consider deprioritizing them. There is freedom in letting go. Keep in mind that delegation can be assigned to those whom you live with first, then consider looking outside if you still need more hands.

Many hands make light work. You are not meant to do and be all things. It is important to be acutely aware of what you have on your plate and then even more so what you can maintain. We often have a disconnect between these two things. Our demands can far outweigh our available supply levels. You must continually remind yourself you can't do it all. We all have commitments that pull us in many directions, but when we name our priorities, it will help us to better know what we need to be most focused on. Protect your schedule and you'll be able to better maintain your home. Focusing well results in living well and living in an organized home.

Takeaways to Take Back Your Home

- How do you feel at the end of most days? Are you burnt out or do you feel accomplished? Are you happy with your schedule and pace?

- What commitments are you obligated to which you could consider saying no to and/or adjusting in some manner? Circles and Bolts don't be too pressured into doing things that don't align with your values and/or energy.

- Where could you outsource some of your daily responsibilities? Or what things could you consider realigning? Ask a Diamond or an Arrow who they use for help. I'm sure they will have great recommendations!

Chapter Four
Experiences

"Turn your wounds
into wisdom."

—Oprah Winfrey

When someone asks me what I do for work and I tell them, "I'm a professional organizer," I typically hear one of two responses. The first is, *"Oh I need you in my life!"* The second is, *"So what is that exactly?"*

The role of a professional organizer can be complex. Professional organizers around the world operate all different forms of businesses. Some companies work exclusively in kitchens and pantries, others provide packing and moving services, and some specifically focus on designing curated and custom-built closets. There are many like me who work as solo entrepreneurs, and others with large teams available to handle any size of project. Regardless of the business model, professional organizers *show up*. We serve as accountability coaches, we help our clients get the work they need to get completed, done. In our organizing toolkits we bring compassion, understanding, efficiency, and tried and true methods to assist with processing any category of "stuff." When someone contacts us, it is often because they have reached the end of their rope. They feel stuck, overwhelmed, and don't know where to start. This means we then get the privilege to help our clients learn how to get started with their organizing, and more importantly, how to keep going.

Bill's daughter Melissa had urged him to contact a professional organizer. She had seen his disorder firsthand, been forced to live amongst his clutter, and witnessed the toll it took on her father. He had just relocated from South Carolina to Colorado and Melissa knew he needed to make a change with how he set up and maintained his living spaces. Bill had also recently retired from teaching, gone through a divorce, and left his four-bedroom house and moved into a two-bedroom apartment. With all the changes and stressors, he was grappling with where to put all his belongings from his previous home and classroom. He had also made a commitment to himself that with his change of address, he would change how he lived in his new home. He desired for his new space to be more cohesive and calming and wanted to get everything processed and unpacked before his son arrived for a visit.

In his previous home, he had often avoided going home because he didn't like living amongst his clutter. Bill had unintentionally created an unorganized home and the excess stuff caused him stress. So, now with a fresh start in a new city and space, he didn't want to repeat those same patterns. He had made the choice to get rid of many of his belongings before relocating to Colorado and had made up his mind he was going to move into a new way of living. He wanted his home to be more organized. So, following Melissa's suggestion, he had hired someone else to help him with his unpacking and decluttering. However, that person had not returned as promised and he was stressed with the amount of work that still needed to be addressed. That's when he reached out to me. I could tell he was in a state of distress and thankfully I could squeeze him into my schedule for an organizing session.

Bill and I met at his apartment on a Sunday afternoon in July. During that first session together, we dove right in and got to organizing. We unpacked boxes, set up his hall closet with labeled containers, and categorized his cherished memories into large storage bins. I insisted he move away from using cardboard boxes and instead store his belongings in transparent bins and/or labeled bins. His previous habit had been to keep things in cardboard boxes in commingled ways and this had only added to his chaos. Bill told me, *"Ditching the boxes ended up being huge for me."* We shifted his spaces from cluttered to categorized and I could sense his feelings of relief. I was honored to be allowed into his home and life.

Using containers from The Dollar Tree was the perfect fit for Bill's hall closet. This was where we set up the bins into zones of like with like items.

> Melissa was recently visiting me, and she thought I should replace a dimming light bulb in my guest bathroom. I pointed her to the hall closet, where the labeled bins are organized and where there is a bin labeled "light bulbs." Melissa instantly came out holding a bulb high and exclaiming (she loves to make exaggerated statements), *"That's the best experience I've ever had anywhere finding a light bulb!"* (I'm also reminded of her pleasure and relief when she first arrived at my place right before Christmas following the summer I had moved. She said to me, *"And I thought I'd be roughing it."*)
>
> —Bill

We have spent a lot of time on paper organization. Organizing paper is more challenging because it is more detailed. To help Bill with paper processing I had him set up clipboards to sort his incoming mail and papers. One clipboard held papers with his to-do items and another clipboard held papers with information needed for the present time (coupons, invites, reminders). We worked to create a system where he would have designated spots to place any category of incoming paper. He needed a visual system for anything requiring his attention and a filing system for papers needing to be retained. I encouraged him to opt for digital delivery with statements. We worked to establish a routine for him to pick up his mail on set days and process it first thing when he returns home. The option to set papers down and let them pile up was off the table, literally. He wanted to keep his dining room table clear so he could write and work on projects; therefore, these steps were critical to help him realize this outcome.

Bill worked diligently to use the systems and strategies we created, but paper continued to be a challenge. He still wrestled with processing his incoming papers and they continued to pile up. He was frustrated by this reality, and I knew we needed to further examine why, when working with paper, he continued to hit a snag. He eventually revealed to me, after digging deeper into his feelings, that those incoming papers and delivered mail reminded him of two things. One was when he used to live more disorganized, he would miss payment due dates for his expenses because he hadn't sorted his mail on time. He would then be required to pay late fees which only added more stress to an already stressful pattern. Secondly, he had memories of seeing and hearing his parents' discussions over finances. They had modeled to him a high level of stress surrounding paperwork. Paper processing wasn't something he had a positive association with. His association with incoming papers had little to do with what he now must open and sort, but to him the papers continued to hold a lot of weight because of past experiences. He didn't see a stack of coupons, marketing flyers, and credit card applications (which is what I see when I get my mail). Instead, he was flooded with the what ifs and what had been. The examples of his past were showing up in his present. Once he was finally able to spotlight the "why" behind his paper problems, he could then open the door to address the habits. He had to reshape his thoughts around paper and reframe his attitude and approach.

Organizing Paper Guidelines [2]

- One Month: deposit/ATM slips, receipts (non-deductible items), reconciled bank statements

- Three Years: mortgage statements, paycheck stubs, expired insurance records, banking checking/savings ledgers

- Seven Years: state and federal tax returns, annual mortgage interest statements, charitable contributions, tax deduction receipts, business/work documents (income and expenses), mileage records, canceled checks, real estate tax forms/records, medical bills/statements

- Forever: automobile titles, contracts, mortgages/property agreements, passports, birth certificates, marriage/divorce papers, active insurance policies, receipts from major purchases (for insurance purposes), wills, educational records, medical records, pension/retirement plans, investment statements

Within the organizing process, there is not a one-size-fits-all approach. In fact, I often tell my clients I don't want to teach them how to organize like I do. I want to teach them how to organize in the ways that will work for them. It is a process of adapting and pivoting to find the best organizing systems, but when you do it, it's a game-changer! For Bill's paper organizing strategy, it took us several attempts to find the right system. My final suggestion was for Bill to set a microwave timer for five minutes and block off that time to

---

[2] This list is provided courtesy of Morganize with Me, LLC. It has been prepared for informational purposes only, and is not intended to provide, and should not be relied on for, tax, legal, or accounting advice.

focus on addressing and processing his paper. He could keep resetting the timer for additional time as required. The best news is that this worked! It took some trial and error, but the time was the ticket. Setting a timer serves as an accountability tool for Bill and his table remains clear.

Another example of organizing adaptability (remember to find the sweet spot between being fixed and flexible) was Bill's closet off his kitchen. I initially let him have this as a catch-all space, but as he improved his spaces throughout his home, we eventually addressed that closet too. I encouraged him to consolidate things into categories and keep everything visual. When things become hidden, they are then more likely to pile up and become a problem of disorganization. For Bolts and Circles, keep things visual and you will keep things maintained.

This was Bill's closet off his kitchen where I gave him some leeway and encouraged him to keep his inventory levels in check. A large space like this can quickly get out of control!

Our life experiences play a significant role in why and how we do things. What we witness then forms the foundations from which we work. We have a lens we look through based on our past experiences. Some have been because of our personal choices and others from other people's choices. What you must identify is what examples or experiences have shaped you and impacted your ability (positively or negatively) to get and stay organized? Has something in your past influenced your organizing efforts in the present? Experiences in our lives can either be building blocks or stumbling blocks. Examine what blocks have framed your foundation and let's work to move any negativity out of the equation.

> **Keep things visual and you will keep things maintained.**

Healthy Experiences

I mentioned earlier my parents were good role models on how to create an organized home. In fact, I don't know what it's like to live in a chaotic home. I feel incredibly grateful for this example and the tone they set for me. I loved that we could "live" in our home. We could kick off shoes, toss things on the counters, and snuggle up with cozy blankets on the couch. Our rooms weren't pristine or perfect, but you can be assured that if I needed to find something I could find it! My feelings of my childhood home are warmth, coziness, comfort, and stability. From a young age I was taught how to clean bathrooms, fold laundry, and keep my room tidy. My sisters and I were held accountable to do chores on a regular basis. I was modeled how to live with routine and responsibility, but with an even greater emphasis on making others feel welcome. Our home was inviting and loving, and so for me, this is what I've wanted to build my home management style upon. I don't want my kids to feel like certain rooms are off-limits or they can't make a mess. Because, if we can't "live" in our homes then what's the point?

Nonetheless, I do want to be transparent and say that my kids (who are now all young adults) tell me I get rid of too many things. While I do *try* to seek permission before I donate things, as the gatekeeper there *have* been times when I will recycle or donate something simply for the sake of my sanity. I realize my kids don't have the same life experiences and still have a lot of life ahead of them. They haven't had to move all their belongings from one home to the next like I have had to do all too many times! All this to say, I hope I'm modeling the examples of intentional consumerism and creating a home that is a place of refuge. I've worked to provide what was given to me. A home where you can be yourself, let down your guard, and find what you need when you need it!

My encouragement is to work to acknowledge the positive and healthy experiences you've had in your life. Who has shown you what good organization looks like? What is an example you'd like to replicate in your home? How can you be a healthy example to your loved ones or roommates? We all can *show up* well, let's commit to doing so.

Experiences in our lives can either be building blocks or stumbling blocks.

Unhealthy Experiences

If you find yourself on the other end of the continuum and have had experiences that have laid a different foundation. Maybe one without much structure, order, or routine, you can work to undo the patterns that have impacted you. You get to decide a new path forward and you can rebuild your foundation.

My recommendation is to first identify what unhealthy experiences were modeled to you. Then spend time exploring your feelings around these memories. A great tool is to journal about your feelings. Let everything out! Express the depth of how the different examples have impacted how you feel and respond today. It is necessary to unpack your feelings and work to move through them. If you don't, your ability to develop new patterns of organization and home management will likely be harder to realize. You can start today and set up new patterns in your life. Work to name your triggers and seek accountability where you need it most. We all have wounds, but it's what we do with the wounding that matters most.

Any organizing shape can be affected by life experiences. I shared in this chapter about family of origin, but experiences can range from a memory at school to something from the workplace or to a friend who has impacted your life in some way. Experiences are healthy if they are good experiences!

Work to be a healthy example and shake off any of the unhealthy examples that have impacted your way of life.

It's been over five years since Bill and I had that first organizing session. I still connect with him from time to time. We check in a few times a year, and he will schedule an in-person "check-in" organizing session with me when he wants extra accountability. This is often before someone visits him because he wants to continue to put his best foot forward. He wants to show his friends and family when they stay with him, his home is organized and uncluttered (which it is!). His apartment has become his refuge, a place of rest, and a place he wants to be. We've also worked on his car organization as this was a second living space for him and had also been a source of stress. He had felt defeated with his car organization, but after a few sessions of reorganizing his car and creating better systems, he can now keep it maintained.

Car Organization Tips

- Treat your car like any other living space. Tidy as you go.

- Every time you return home, bring things in and put them back in their homes.

- Add a spot to corral garbage and only keep essentials in your car.

- Designate zones: car info, tissues, chargers, sunglasses, kids' stuff, etc.

- In the trunk, add containment to help store those items that you must keep in your car: snow chains, battery cable chargers, blankets, and reusable shopping bags, for example.

Bill knew he wanted to start fresh with his new habits and practices, but he also acknowledged that he could benefit from some added accountability and assistance. With Melissa's prompting he reached out to me, and I was honored and grateful for the opportunity to coach him. Your home should always be a place you want to return to.

Takeaways to Take Back Your Home

- What does "living" in your home look like to you? How do you want your home to look and feel?

- What examples/habits do you want to start doing/modeling? And what examples/habits do you want to stop doing/modeling?

- Have you ever practiced journaling? This is a great tool that can help you peel back the layers of the organizing onion and see which area(s) may remain a stumbling block for you.

Chapter Five
Purchases

"The odds of going to the store for a loaf of bread and coming out with only a loaf of bread are three billion to one."

—Erma Bombeck, bestselling author and American humorist

My number one tip for staying organized is to become an "intentional shopper." An intentional shopper shops with a plan and is purposeful. They make shopping lists, know their home inventory, and regularly reset their spaces. I know these steps can be hard to prioritize and maintain. I too struggle to shop intentionally. If I am shopping and I feel hungry, stressed, or can't find what I'm looking for, I'll make poor choices and purchase things with less thought and intent. I also won't pretend to suggest I haven't been swayed to buy the neck cream on social media that everyone raved about. Most of us are guilty of picking up items because they are "on sale" or adding more things to our online carts to avoid paying shipping costs. From appliances to clothes to technology, we are devoted consumers. We like to consume things and shopping is more accessible than ever. Convenient yes, but so is the potential to overspend and over acquire.

In 1930, the average American woman owned nine outfits. Today, that figure is thirty outfits—one for every day of the month.[3] I would argue most women I know (me included) have far more than thirty outfits. Let's face it—we are all influenced constantly by persuasive marketing and fabulous BOGO deals. For the longest time, I couldn't figure out why I was seeing BOGO everywhere. I thought it must be a new brand I hadn't heard of! Well, my daughter informed me it meant buy one, get one free. Obviously. But what if I don't even need one of something?

Stacey reached out to me because another client of mine (Courtney, who you will hear from later) had suggested Stacey contact me. However, it took Stacey a few years to muster up the courage to call. I think her final push was when her therapist suggested she do so. Like many of my clients, she had arrived at the place where she was tired of feeling stuck and was buried under her stuff. She was ready to make a change and wanted to take back her home. Her call to me was her first of many hard steps. I could tell from our initial conversation that Stacey felt shame and was frustrated with her situation. She desperately wanted to pave a new path forward.

Stacey had developed a habit of moving belongings to her primary bedroom or closet when she didn't have the time or energy to deal with them. Rather than moving items back to where they may belong, she combined things into

---

3   Johnson, Emma, "The Real Cost of Your Shopping Habits," January 15, 2016, Forbes.com, www.forbes.com/sites/emmajohnson/2015/01/15/the-real-cost-of-your-shopping-habits/?sh=4cfd86ec1452.

boxes and bags and shoved them into her room or closet with the intent that they would be dealt with later. She put them away, but not in the places where they belonged. Please note we can *all* fall into this tendency. Our time is pressed with priorities and our days are full of constant interruptions. Nevertheless, small choices like these in the moment to avoid clutter usually multiply our clutter and the stress surrounding it. One indecision becomes a multitude of indecisions. When things start unraveling, we are then more inclined to provide permission for the full unravel. This is what had happened to Stacey. She had postponed sorting and putting things away and was now sinking under too much stuff. She was also grappling with her kids getting older and the shifting of the seasons.

To start processing her piles, we had to work in small, deliberate sections. There was a lot of sorting to do, and it took an increased amount of time and attention because many of the items were tossed together with little to no categorization. I was concerned about how much progress we could make because the amount of stuff was daunting, but Stacey was committed! After our first few organizing sessions, her primary bedroom had regained its space and the room felt tranquil.

One day while working together, I asked her more about what had led to the buildup of all the unprocessed stuff. She shared with me that in her childhood she hadn't been provided with much extra in material ways, and therefore, when she could shop more freely and with greater resources, she fell into a pattern of purchasing without purpose. She was making up for lost time by buying things she could now afford. The piles of things had much less to do with the "stuff" and much more to do with her deeper feelings and emotions. She was trying to comfort the feelings she had endured as a child. Feelings likely of comparison to others, vulnerability, or even jealousy. Hearing her backstory gave me more understanding and compassion for what we were wading through. It helped me to better know what else we needed to work on and through. We went on to talk through what strategies she could implement to be a more intentional shopper and what this would be like for her.

She said she would begin by using up the numerous shampoo and conditioner bottles she had already purchased. She also committed to stop purchasing items unless she needed to buy things that required replenishing.

Stacey committed to knowing her home inventory and then shopping based on needs versus wants. Simple in theory; however, more difficult in practice. I mean, the marketing gurus are good!

Many of my clients who also have an abundance of stuff in their homes, now as adults, often share a similar past to Stacey's. Often, we will overcompensate with certain choices in our lives because we didn't have specific wants or needs met as we desired them to be met when we were younger. Therefore, when we become more independent or when we can change our situation, we do so. But unfortunately, we often act and then overact! These layered experiences, positive and negative, run deep and can be hard to name and process. And it's incredibly challenging to undo years of influencing and messaging. But the first step is to acknowledge it, which is what Stacey did. She started, like we all should, with baby steps. If unintentional and casual purchasing has contributed to more chaos in your home and you feel overwhelmed, you can make a change! Here are three tools you can begin to implement into your home and life today.

Shopping Lists

Make it a practice to keep a list of the things you need to buy. Use any form you prefer—digital, sticky notes, your planner, a notepad. List everything and in different categories. I like to have an ongoing list of clothing items I need for my closet so I can better complete outfits. My husband and I coordinate our menu planning by making the weekly grocery list together. As things come up that we need, we jot them down. Noting what you need when you run out of something or coordinating your upcoming schedule with your shopping plans will help you minimize mental clutter. It will allow you to let go of trying to remember everything all the time. There's enough to remember day-to-day without trying to keep track of items you need for a recipe or a specific clothing piece for your closet. Then to shop more productively (and save time, money, and energy), bring your list with you and create a strategy for your buying.

This may look like shopping weekly for your groceries online and scheduling pick up or delivery. You may make it a goal to go to the warehouse store and stock up on your bigger box items only once a month. Or decide to set up a monthly or quarterly budget for your clothing needs and then commit to not overspending. Remember when you shop that every item you purchase will take up space in your home and more mental space too. All our belongings require our attention and take time to process. When we shop without a strategy and a list, it can be easy to overload our homes with stuff we don't need, which then leads to increased feelings of stress and anxiety.

> One organizing hack that encourages implementation is an ongoing shopping list "template" for regularly purchased items. Those grocery and household items you need to shop for weekly and monthly. Creating a set list will save you time to compile your lists and keep you focused on what you need to shop for. This is a hack I learned from my mom and it's a game changer when it comes to getting your list complied quickly and efficiently. I'm sharing a sample below of my grocery list template that I created. I also designed it in the pattern I move through my grocery store. This is efficiency in practice! See an example of the one I use below. (Of course, I copied this from my mom; she paved the way.)

Menu & Shopping List

Produce	Baking	Dairy & Meat	Frozen
[ ]	[ ]	[ ]	[ ]
[ ]	[ ]	[ ]	[ ]
[ ]	[ ]	[ ]	[ ]
[ ]	[ ]	[ ]	[ ]
[ ]	[ ]	[ ]	[ ]
[ ]	[ ]	[ ]	[ ]
[ ]	[ ]	[ ]	[ ]
[ ]	[ ]	[ ]	[ ]
[ ]	[ ]	[ ]	[ ]
[ ]	[ ]	[ ]	[ ]

Pasta & Breads	Pantry Staples	Beverages	Household
[ ]	[ ]	[ ]	[ ]
[ ]	[ ]	[ ]	[ ]
[ ]	[ ]	[ ]	[ ]
[ ]	[ ]	[ ]	[ ]
[ ]	[ ]	[ ]	[ ]
[ ]	[ ]	[ ]	[ ]
[ ]	[ ]	[ ]	[ ]
[ ]	[ ]	[ ]	[ ]
[ ]	[ ]	[ ]	[ ]
[ ]	[ ]	[ ]	[ ]

Menu Plan (Day/Date)	Breakfast/Lunch	Dinner	Other

Stock Management

Next, ensure you know your home inventory. The more attention you pay to keeping up with your stock and backstock, the less energy you'll spend planning, purchasing, and resetting. When you know what's in your fridge, pantry, cupboards, and closets, you'll know what you need to buy. I cannot begin to tell you how many times I've uncovered five or more spice bottles of the same seasoning, or dozens of rolls of Christmas gift wrap in July, or perfectly good cleaning products in the back of a cupboard that had been long since been forgotten about. Keeping track of your inventory takes time and knowing what you have in back stock requires effort, but it is worth it. You will avoid buying duplicates and triplicates. You will save yourself an extra trip to the store to buy a tool you already own. You will avoid throwing away expired foods and waste less. I call this shopping sustainably.

When you manage your inventory, it will help you better prioritize buying what you need when you need it. So, if you find yourself being swayed by a great deal or feel an emotional tug to buy something, double-check your list, consider what's in your backstock, and know that if it's not listed you don't need it.

Fridge labels are by no means necessary, but they can help so that everyone knows where things go!

System Resets

Your commitment to intentional shopping doesn't end at the checkout. Whether the box was delivered to your doorstep, or you had to lug the reusable bags into your home—there are always next steps. And these next steps are some of the most important ones you'll take.

When you go to unpack your purchases, it is critical to do a "reset." This will look like decanting items, rotating products by expiration dates, tossing what needs to go, and recycling all packaging. This will also encompass noting what things you need to add to your next shopping list. It's an ongoing effort to keep your systems maintained and the best way to do so is to do regular resets. I encourage you to build in time when you return home from shopping—specifically, grocery shopping (as there is usually more to process with food items). Block off fifteen to thirty minutes to clean out your fridge, take out the trash, and put everything in place in its home. If you don't have dedicated "homes" yet, it's okay, we'll get to this. For now, put things *like with like* as much as possible. The more you stay on the resetting train the better! When you do, you can create specific shopping lists, follow through with your strategies, and better know and maintain your stock levels.

Look over your backstock *before* you go shopping; note what you need more of and only add those items to your shopping list.

Lastly, I want to share that Stacey moved mountains with her home decluttering and reorganizing. The dedication she had to work through her clutter was tremendous! She shared with me she was only buying what she needed at the store and could feel the difference in her home. The day she texted me a photo of a huge row of donation boxes lined up on her driveway for pickup, I couldn't help but smile from ear to ear. Stacey had strategically shifted from mindlessly buying to intentional shopping, and her home and peace of mind revealed the results. We must shop and purchase items for our daily lives. There is no way we can avoid this necessary task, but we can become intentional shoppers. Our organizing efforts start and stop with our shopping carts. You are the steward of your wants and needs, so take charge. To further help with our efforts to shop intentionally, I'm considering making a t-shirt that says, *"Intentionally Shopping Until I Drop!"* Of course they will be marketed as BOGO.

Our organizing efforts start and stop with our shopping carts.

Takeaways to Take Back Your Home

- In what areas do you tend to over-shop or overindulge? Why is this? What has contributed to this tendency?

- If you are a Bolt or a Circle you might find buying with purpose more challenging and if so, work to build in better strategies and boundaries to help you steer through the aisles (no pun intended; well, maybe a little).

- Want less? You must buy less. If you desire more clean surfaces and want your cabinets to have more breathing room, you must bring home less and/or let go of more. Our front doors are revolving doors, and we are the gatekeepers. I challenge you to be a good gatekeeper.

Chapter Six

Memories

"Memory is the diary we all carry about with us."

—Oscar Wilde

Part II: Organizing Snags   87

You know the feeling when you meet someone, and you realize right away they are the type of person who is going to make you a better person? Well, this sums up my dear friend Tiffany. She is enthusiastic, fun, and creative. Everything she does, she does with excellence. I've been referred to as an "energizer bunny," but, guaranteed, Tiffany would beat me at any race! She has run thirty-nine marathons and has no plans on stopping. Talk about dedication! She can't help but to encourage and inspire you to be your best.

Several years ago, she called and asked me to help her with organizing some spaces in her stunning lakeside home. How could I resist? Our daughters introduced us to each other, but little did we know it would be the beginning of a great friendship. Tiffany and her husband, both busy professionals, had been living life to the fullest and raising their two children, which had naturally led to some accumulation. From hobbies, to travels, to sports and more, Tiffany was feeling buried in all the stuff and wanted to create more breathing room. She was ready to declutter several spaces in her home. (Typically, with every additional person, life change, or activity, the result is that more things are added.)

Yes, her race medals are organized and on display. As important memories should be!

The irony though, is now that I am friends with Tiffany, I have discovered she is one of the most organized people I have ever met! My favorite example of her organizing skills is that every year she commits to taking one picture a day. The snapshot is a highlight of her day and then she posts the picture to her private Instagram account, one that no one else sees. At the end of the year, she makes a chat book with a picture highlighted for every single day of the year. I absolutely love this idea, but I am hesitant to try and do this myself because I know I'll end up missing a day (or ten) and then feel stuck. Not Tiffany; she gets it done.

While working together to declutter her basement storage area, I was amazed at the rows and rows of scrapbooks and photo albums. I had never seen such a commitment to a craft or so many memories so beautifully documented. It motivated me to get home and work on my photo organization! (Please tell me I'm not the only one guilty of stockpiling years of unorganized photos on my phone?) As we organized together and got to know one another better, Tiffany shared with me how her father's recent passing had inspired her to take a closer look at her belongings and all the memories she had accumulated. Looking at all the stuff neatly tucked away in her basement had her questioning why she had saved so much of it. Why had she prioritized documenting and preserving so many memories? How much money and time had she spent? And did she make the time to look through things and reminisce? (All good questions to consider.)

Have you ever seen anything more impressive? Talk about documentation! So many memories and smiles, all artistically arranged. (And this is only some of them!)

Over the years, she had created photo albums (scrapbooks) for her children, one for each year of their life. So, now that they were in high school, the grand total was nearing thirty-six embellished and custom-made scrapbooks! There were also specialty cake pans for every birthday year. They had a family tradition of baking a special cake for each birthday and it was always a different theme. So fun! This is a great and memorable tradition, but now she was also left storing over thirty specialty cake pans. I told her maybe she should consider opening a bakery! I'd be the first person in line for the carrot cake.

As we worked through the basement shelves, Tiffany did a great job of sorting and making tough decisions quickly. At the end of each session, I would pack my SUV to the brim and take everything to the donation center. She was determined to minimize and downsize, but the organizing process was also leading her to question why she had gone so big with all the memory-making and preservation in the first place. As we talked further, she pinpointed that some of it was likely to make up for some lack of memory-making in her childhood. But some of it was also because of who she is. She desires to live life to the fullest and wants to capture everything in photos and memories. And walking through the loss of her father provided a new lens for her to look through and examine things. She still wanted to prioritize making memories, but she also wanted to refocus and minimize how much stuff she would keep organized and stored.

Our lives are made up of memories and we must work to strike a balance between the past, present, and future. We are constantly moving between these three spaces in time, and no collection of "stuff" will slow down or speed up the process. We need to aim somewhere in the middle.

Your Past

We all have happy and special memories that we want to hold on to, and deciding how much to keep and what to let go of is where the tension lies. Often, we don't want to part with items that were a significant part of our memory-making experience. We can feel the items associated with the memory need to be physically kept for us to remember. Or we may want to save items to share with the next generation. I personally have a hope chest my dad built for me, and it has both my and my husband's memories tucked inside. It has yearbooks, cards, the outfits each of our babies wore home from the hospital, and more. There are things I want to keep in my hope chest forever. I hope I'm in a rocking chair someday trying to remember my high school classmates' names, laughing at the pictures and styles of yesteryear while flipping through my old yearbooks. The yearbooks are important to me. But not everything can be important. We must make choices.

What the hope chest does for us, is it creates a boundary. A boundary can be any defined space and naming this is an important first step to creating an organized system. For example, if we can't shut the hope chest, which hasn't happened yet, we would then need to go through and cull things. It's important to have a place where you can place those items you cherish, but ensure it is a manageable-sized space. I don't want to hear you rented a storage unit to house all your childhood memories. As I shared in Chapter 2, if you value something, make it a priority to be something you can access and use. If it's tucked away and never used or appreciated, then I must ask you, how much do you value it? This doesn't apply to all things, but it does to many things.

Let's say you have fancy fine China that has been passed down to you and you've been storing it for decades, but you never actually use it. Then I would ask, why are you keeping it? Do you truly value it? While the dishes may be memorable from past shared holiday gatherings or special to your family members, this doesn't mean you need to keep them stored (and never used). The memories are not in the pretty plates; they are in your heart. I say this, realizing you may need to keep items out of a commitment or obligation to someone else. And in these situations, I recommend honoring and respecting others more than stuff. However, this should go both ways and remember this too when you pass something on to someone else. Let a gift be a gift with no strings or obligations attached.

Let a gift be a gift, with no strings or obligations attached.

Your Present

I'm a forward thinker and thus tend to look more toward the future than feel content in the moment. While some of these tendencies are helpful and can keep me on track, I also realize I can be guilty of missing magical moments because I am overly concerned with what's next. This pattern can be easy to fall into. Diamonds and Arrows are likely to have a harder time staying in the present as they tend to look more toward the future. Circles and Bolts are likely to be more naturally present but can also fall into the habit of hanging on too tightly to their pasts and memories. Their heartstrings often get tugged more easily.

My encouragement when it comes to living in the "now" is to make living in your current season of life your aim. Your time is now, and you will never get today back. In my book *Take Back Your Time,* I share about our life seasons and how crucial it is to recognize your current life season. In each chapter of your life, your obligations and responsibilities are unique. Different parts of your life require different things from you. You aren't meant to do all things all the time. Identifying your purposes for your current life season is a great place to start. Then work to prioritize those things that fall under those purposes first and foremost. When you are clear with what you need to focus on you can more effectively use your time and energies on your top priorities.

When working with my clients with young children, I often share that the season they are currently in will pass. I know they feel exhausted from tripping over toys and stepping on sharp Lego pieces, but one day they may miss these realities! It's hard to imagine missing something that feels annoying in the present, but the past will often represent itself more fondly. I say this to them to give them permission to accept the playroom as it is. Yes, it's now bursting with toys and feels chaotic, but these circumstances won't last forever. Nor will the messing fingerprints all over the counter tops. Their countertops will likely all too quickly be replaced with car keys and cell phones. Life is a bittersweet experience. Work to commit to living fully now, accepting what is, and adjusting what needs to be changed. Stay present and allow your home to serve your needs and your loved one's needs, simply for today.

Your Future

For Tiffany, one question we needed to explore was why she was still holding on to all those cake pans. The cake pans had served their intended purpose. She had purchased them, baked the cakes, and celebrated the birthdays. Of course, she also has beautiful photos of her children blowing out their candles on these custom-made cakes. So, the question to explore was if she could make the choice to let them go. The answer was yes and no.

Tiffany recognized that the cake pans had served their purpose, and she had the memories documented. Nonetheless, she also stated she had a dream of using the cake pans hopefully with future grandchildren. I love this! What a fun tradition to look forward to and, knowing Tiffany, I know she will fulfill this dream. In this case, looking forward to the future helped her to make the best decision for today. She did part with several of the cake pans and only kept the most meaningful ones for future memory-making. This is what you want to consider: always think of the big picture. Use the future you desire to be the benchmark for how you set things up for yourself now. When we ignore the big picture, it often pulls us back to the past and keeps us stuck in nostalgia.

Tiffany has her cake pans organized and stored. This is a #morganized approved system and I respect her priority in keeping these special pans. I can't wait to see the grandbaby photos!

When we possess too much, we can miss the opportunity to share the potential gifts or usability with someone else. Storing things (you are not using) that could be used by someone else might be a wonderful gift to both you and the receiver. Not only will you clear up space and responsibility, but the receiver will also get to use something with a present value to them. If an item or collection no longer serves you, be willing to move on. Time is a gift. We must protect it while also looking forward to another candle each year on our birthday cake!

Organizing a Keepsake Box

A common challenge for parents is knowing what to do with all their children's papers. My suggestion is a "Keepsake Box." A Keepsake Box will store your child's memory items within a paper range size of 8.5 x 11 inches or less. For larger items, paper and otherwise (trophies, artwork, etc.) consider also designating a larger bin for those types of things. Typically, kids will bring home an *assortment* of keepsake items, things that they *really* want to keep!

Here is a general list of categories/files you can use to create a Keepsake Box. Select the top twenty-five categories that best apply to your child and their needs. Or feel free to keep a few unlabeled blank files, this way as their hobbies and/or interests evolves and change, you can make the necessary additions. You may also combine files, for example putting each year's report card in the corresponding year. What's most important is to make the system work for you and your precious child.

- Infant
- Toddler
- Preschool
- Kindergarten
- First through twelfth grade (one file for each)
- Report cards
- Academic awards
- Athletic awards
- Sports (specific categories or general)
- Misc.
- Clubs (specific categories or general)
- Activities (specific categories or general)
- Birthdays
- Cards (holiday/birthday—may have multiple files)
- Artwork
- Pictures
- Hobbies
- Medical

A Keepsake Box will store your child's memory items within a paper range size of 8.5 x 11 inches.

Takeaways to Take Back Your Home

- Where do you get stuck with living in the past and/or holding on to memories with your possessions? What would it look like for you if you looked more toward the future?

- Bolts and Circles: work to place as much emphasis on letting things go as you do with bringing things in. Arrows and Diamonds: don't be too quick to move on from one thing to the next. Savor the special moments and make a priority to experience the beautiful memories!

- The big picture is your aim! Consider how you want things to look and feel. What do you want to remember and what is most meaningful to you? Everything cannot hold the same importance. Prioritize and align everything up with your intentional priorities and purposes.

Chapter 7

Abilities

"There are three ways to ultimate success: The first way is to be kind. The second way is to be kind. The third way is to be kind."

—Mister Rogers

Prior to relocating to Colorado, Debbie had been working as a traveling nurse, a job she loved and was passionate about. She could see different parts of the country and meet all kinds of people. While working that job, she kept her three-bedroom home in Texas as her home base. She enjoyed coming and going, working wherever she was called to. All was going well for her, until she was diagnosed with an ulcer in 2018. This then meant she had to immediately stop working and go on disability. It was hard for Debbie to suddenly pivot from a career she loved and be unable to physically work. This unexpected change in her career also meant she needed to adjust her living situation.

Her son, Andy, talked with her and encouraged her to downsize to a two-bedroom apartment. He thought she should work to let go of 75 percent of her stuff. To Debbie this felt daunting, and she didn't know where to start. (This would feel daunting to me too!) Andy was looking out for her best interests and wanted his mom to live more comfortably, both physically and financially. However, for Debbie, downsizing her possessions would be tough physical and emotional work. Her stuff equaled her life. All her belongings represented a lifetime of her precious experiences and memories. Choosing which belongings to part with would not be an easy decision. At that time, she began the process of decluttering, but it was a large-scale project.

Her stuff equaled her life.

Several years later, she still had a lot of work to do but she had decided to move to Fort Collins, Colorado, where Andy and his family had moved. This is where I came in. Debbie needed help. Not only was she still dealing with her disability, but she was now also trying to navigate unpacking and getting moved into her new and even smaller one-bedroom apartment. When we met it had been around six months since Debbie had arrived in Colorado and she was still shuffling around stacks of moving boxes and unprocessed stuff. Using her walker and trying to get through the piles of boxes was difficult. Andy, her son, and Rachel, her daughter-in-law, were tired of witnessing her struggles and wanted to help her get organized. Not only was it stressful, but it was also unsafe. Debbie had worked to part with some belongings prior to moving, but she still needed to address the amount of stuff that she could realistically fit into her new apartment. Downsizing is a process, and it often takes more time and energy than we want to give it.

When I arrived for our first session it was hard to walk through her home. There were small paths, but overall, there were a lot of things stacked and taking up space. In situations like this it can be difficult to know where to start. That day, I suggested we begin with her small storage closet off the patio. This is often a good place to begin, because once you set up your storage spot, as you process other rooms you can move things to your storage space(s) in an organized fashion. I always make it my goal to touch things the least number of times as possible. Beginning with storage spaces often helps with this.

Debbie was ready to do some hard work and make important decisions, but this didn't mean it was easy. She told me, *"It's hard to let go of my things because I worked hard to purchase them, and many are also gifts that have great meaning to me."* This is where there had been some tension between her and Andy and Rachel. They wanted her to live in a safe environment and were encouraging her to shift toward a simpler way of living, ultimately for her health and well-being. They desired for her to be comfortable in her new home and feel settled, but they had gotten frustrated with trying to help. They were so close to her and the challenges, so it made things more difficult all around.

I'm happy to report that as a team, Debbie, Rachel, Andy, and I worked hard together. And as a result, Debbie now has a functional and tidy apartment. We went through every single box of papers, memories, photos, decorations, sewing supplies, clothing, you name it. We created "homes" for each category that was a part of Debbie's current life season and got rid of around 50 percent of the things she no longer needed. She did a great job with being both discerning and decisive.

My encouragement to you is for you to believe in yourself. You can live your life more organized! But you need to first go back to where we started; you need to get to the core of *knowing yourself*. Your abilities—emotionally, mentally, and physically—play a role in how you organize, and which snags tend to get in your way. Some stumbling blocks you may allow and others you may not have a say in. Nevertheless, when you work to identify your strengths and weaknesses it will help you to better make the organizational changes you want to make.

Part II: Organizing Snags 99

Rachel and Andy requested organizing help from me for Andy's mom, Debbie. They were a huge help with the entire process. I was touched by how they lovingly stepped in and worked to get Debbie unpacked, decluttered, and more organized. It can be challenging to navigate how to help a loved one downsize and downshift their number of belongings, but the entire family was committed and that's what made the difference!

Briefly explain your experience with Debbie and her patterns of behavior toward her belongings. What have been the challenges?

Rachel: We had made great strides in some areas, for instance, selling a house she no longer needed, canceling cable, and no longer paying for a storage unit. However, when downsizing from a house to a one-bedroom apartment, she was unable to cull many of her belongings, resulting in an extremely cramped space. The apartment was difficult to clean and climbing around boxes or through tight spaces with mobility issues was dangerous for her. It reached a point where we needed to make big changes!

Andy: Even as a child we always had too much "stuff" in our house. I think buying "stuff" provides a brief but powerful dopamine hit and is a tough habit to break (like snacking, or various other bad habits people get themselves into). But the issue looks dramatically worse when you can't (partially) hide the accumulation in extra closets/basements/attics in a larger house or in an additional storage unit.

How have you navigated her tendencies toward accumulation? And how has it impacted you personally?

Rachel: We had done many workdays where we would work for a few hours unloading boxes and getting rid of things, but we were too close to the issue to have much success. It is such a letdown to work for hours and not see much progress. It became a great stressor for my husband as our son grew, he noticed his surroundings when visiting her house. We finally felt unable to handle the stress of the space on our own and are so glad to have enlisted Morgan's help. Her distance from the issue emotionally, and her fresh perspective helped Debbie approach the purging process with an open mind and freely let go of things that she had held onto for too long.

> What advice would you give to someone who has a loved one struggling with clutter or consumption?
>
> **Rachel:** *It isn't about the stuff.* It's about habits and emotions. If you can afford professional help in the form of an organizer or therapist (or both), enlist their help.
>
> **Andy:** Have patience, although it's a big ask. I am not sure we *ever* would have gotten as far as we did without Morgan's help.

Emotionally

One of my favorite tools to help me with naming what I'm feeling emotionally in the moment is to use an Emotions Wheel graphic (see next page). As a logical person by nature, I regularly grapple with specifying what I'm feeling. I will know I feel off but can't quite put my finger on the emotion. This tool helps me to identify the feeling.

When we're feeling discouraged about how to get spaces organized, we can wrestle with feelings of being fearful, angry, or sad. We might be mad because we are stuck with our clutter (or someone else's). There could be feelings of sadness for the memories and seasons that are now only in our rearview mirror. Or we are scared to make decisions about what and how much we should declutter. Rather than shifting toward more positive feelings of joy or love, we feel stressed!

Clients will share with me they don't feel confident in making decisions. They are not sure if they are making the right choices, and this hesitation keeps them stagnant. They avoid saying yes or no, and when they do make a choice, they are usually not clear with their choice. Their decisions are more out of insecurity than confidence. This pattern of decision-making does not propel them forward. I want you to be confident that you can work to declutter and organize. You can make decisions and choices with an attitude of assurance. While it may be hard to start or fall into this rhythm, you are capable.

An Emotions Wheel is a great visual tool you can use to help you identify what you are feeling and experiencing in the moment.

We spend a lot of time thinking through things in our heads. Pondering, stressing, wondering, hoping. While some of these are strengths that help us to process information and act. Other times they can contribute to the feeling as though we are on a hamster wheel. Things keep spinning around and around and it feels as though there is no way to get off. We want to press the reset button, but we can't. It's important to be aware of when you feel indecisive or fearful and then work through these thoughts and feelings as opposed to letting them fester within.

Begin by making a choice to talk kindly to yourself and be gentle too! Our inner dialogue plays a role in how we show up in this big old world. Don't say things to yourself you wouldn't say to someone else. Practice being your own cheerleader. Celebrate the small *and* big victories. Avoid shifting into a shame cycle. You can do better once you have the systems and strategies in place. If it were easy to be organized, everyone would be! If it's a priority for you, make it important. Start with protecting your thoughts and then move toward processing your things. Check in with your heart and your emotions. Notice your responses and what factors contribute to your feelings, both positively and negatively.

As Debbie's daughter-in-law Rachel said it best, "*It isn't about the stuff. It's about habits and emotions.*"

Bolts and Circles can be more emotional with how they approach their organizing, but in general they aren't as hard on themselves. Whereas Arrows and Diamonds tend to be more logical. Whatever your organizing shape, find a way to experience more peace, joy, and power by taking back your home! Feel your feelings and let them motivate you from within.

Mentally

Many of my clients tell me they suspect they have attention deficit hyperactivity disorder (ADHD) or share they have an ADHD diagnosis. Others mention their inclination to hyperfocus or overanalyze, and how they have a hard time moving forward or getting things done. The accumulation of physical stuff and the inability to manage it is often tied to a deeper "why." For many, this might be because of a neurodivergent condition. If someone feels more anxious or has a harder time focusing it can make it more difficult to organize and create structure. A non-medical umbrella term, "*Neurodiversity is the concept that there are a variety of ways that people's brains process information, function, and present behaviorally. Rather than thinking there is something wrong or problematic when some people don't operate similarly to others, neurodiversity embraces all differences.*"[4] Neurodivergent conditions

---

4   Resnick, Ariane, "What Does it Mean to be Neurodivergent," November 2, 2023, Verywellmind.com, www.verywellmind.com/what-is-neurodivergence-and-what-does-it-mean-to-be-neurodivergent-5196627.

often include, but are not limited to: ADHD, obsessive-compulsive disorder (OCD), autism, and dyslexia.

If you can relate to feeling as though your mental abilities or capacities make it harder for you to put your life in order, I want you to know you are not alone! If you are challenged with inattentiveness, high stress levels, or trying to overly control your environments, there are ways to work through these obstacles. Whether or not you have a diagnosis, look for the patterns you repeat and those that aren't helping you with what you want to achieve. Where does your mind go when you try to prioritize? What keeps you stuck? How do you stay focused or what distracts you? Getting organized is tough enough on its own, but if you are maxed out mentally or navigating life with a neurodivergent condition, you can feel defeated before you even get started.

One way to help your mental ability to focus and organize is to find what motivates you. The most challenging piece to getting organized can be finding motivation. I always say it takes a combination of time and motivation, at the same moment. However, these two factors don't usually align together in perfect unison. If you can relate to having a harder time with getting motivated to organize, I encourage you to build in rewards for yourself after you do your organizing work. After all, it is work! So, reward your efforts. Choose only one small space/section, set up a defined amount of time for your project, and then build in a fun treat or activity for when you finish. Doing this will help you to not only get started but then to finish too!

In Part 4—organizing strategies—I will share more tangible tips to help with organizing if you have a neurodivergent condition. There are great strategies if you or a loved one struggles with one of these conditions.

Physically

One snag you or someone you know may have with trying to get organized is a physical limitation. If someone is aging or has a medical condition, they may not have the stamina or mobility to physically manage what needs to be organized. Debbie was in this situation. She couldn't lift and lug her boxes to and from. She couldn't put things high in the cupboards. She relied on her walker to get around and therefore didn't have two free hands to carry belongings. Debbie needed more helping hands.

Know yourself. If you are in a season of your life where you have physical limitations, consider who else you could recruit to help. A good friend who is direct with you would be an excellent choice! They can tell you that you don't need to keep every concert t-shirt from every concert you've ever been to. I'm sure they would be more than happy to help you offload some of your excesses or set up functional systems within your home.

Organizing is physical work. I usually schedule my organizing work with clients in two-to-four-hour sessions. I have found that around the four-hour mark both I and the client hit a wall. We are physically tired from the movement. My clients feel mentally drained from making so many decisions. And emotionally drained from either reliving memories or discovering things we didn't even know had gotten disorganized. (When you start to dig into a project, you often find more beneath the surface than you realized was there.)

Be vulnerable and ask yourself the hard questions. Surround yourself with loved ones who will walk through your organizing work with you. Organizing requires a lot from you emotionally, mentally, and physically. Plan accordingly. Be courageous, name your strengths and weaknesses, and most of all, be gentle with yourself.

When I showed up one day for a session with Debbie, I asked her how she was feeling about the process. She smiled a big smile and told me, *"I feel confident!"* This made my day! She had turned the corner and was no longer stuck holding on to things that no longer served her needs. Debbie did the hard work and prioritized her surroundings. She wanted her home to be a safe place for her and her sweet pup, Maggie.

After lots of teamwork, her home is now a sanctuary! Debbie now wants to have people over, she feels confident, and her home makes her smile. What more can you ask for?

Takeaways to Take Back Your Home

- Do you practice being kind to yourself? Are your thoughts positive toward your efforts? How can you be more gracious with your progress?

- What challenges do you have when it comes to getting motivated to work on organizing? Are there things you can do to better motivate you? Circles and Bolts will need to be more intentional to build in rewards to help them get motivated and stay the course.

- How do your home surroundings make you feel? What do you want to experience in your home? Are you comfortable opening your home to others?

Part III
ORGANIZING SYSTEMS

"HOME IS THE NICEST WORD THERE IS."

—Laura Ingalls Wilder, American author

David and I have been married now for close to thirty years. Over the course of our three decades together we have lived in fourteen different homes. We have set up homes in multiple states and lived overseas in Europe. Our homes have ranged from two-bedroom apartments to three-story homes, to various long-term furnished rentals. From all these relocations, we have become experienced with decluttering, packing, and moving. Thankfully, several of our relocations were determined by a career change and employers provided us with professional movers. However, we have also packed and moved ourselves halfway across the country and we lived to talk about it! Barely.

I have learned from living in so many different homes that every home is unique. What works in one layout doesn't necessarily transfer to the next floorplan, and vice versa. Furniture doesn't fit like it did in the last place, color palettes are different, and storage options usually shift too.

Organizing and setting up a home is a lot like playing the computer game Tetris. If you are unfamiliar with the game, it's a digital game where you must line up each block configuration with the next and get them to fit together in a puzzle formation. To make the patterns connect you must rotate and shift the individual shape to get two or more shapes to align. Creating a functional home takes a similar approach. Keep pivoting and tweaking things to identify the right fit. And it's usually not effortless or a smooth process. You might feel as though you are taking one step forward and two steps back with every project you attempt. But take heart: it doesn't have to feel or be this way!

As you learned from Bill, he turned his home into his happy place. Debbie decluttered and unpacked, which helped her transition from chaos to calm. And Stacey made a commitment to stop over buying which contributed to her home being more peace-filled and less stuff-filled. It takes work to create a home that both serves and sustains you. I want the word "home" to be the nicest word you can think of. It should be the place where you retreat to in order to relax and recharge.

> **It takes work to create a home that both serves and sustains you.**

To make this a reality we'll go room by room, looking at seven common spaces within a home. The spaces are called storing, cooking, living, bathing, clothing, playing/working, and sleeping. I purposely chose words for the rooms and spaces that end in "-ing." The -ing ending means *continuous action*. Yes, you will get a space reset and establish systems, but you will also need to commit to regular maintenance. View your home organization as an ongoing process that will require ongoing attention and action. This is the key to *staying* organized!

In this section we will explore what creating organized systems looks like. This is the "how-to," the application, the time when you will get things done! Consider as you approach each space which organizing snags may present for you and then try to get in front of those hurdles. Also, play to the strengths of your organizing shape. Your style needs to be honored as you work to organize. If a space doesn't resonate with you, you will likely still be able to pick up some tangible and transferable tips.

Use this book as your toolbox. Pick up the specific tool you need for today. If your bathroom is a disaster, jump to Chapter 11. Do you have zero clue of where to start? Go to the first space I suggest you work on (storage areas), which are highlighted in Chapter 8. I'll explain why when you get there. Maybe you are sick and tired of not finding a system to put your clothes away easily. Then I suggest you flip to Chapter 12, where I break down my clothing and closet organizing systems. Getting dressed everyday should *not* need to make you feel stressed!

Before moving ahead, please read through the following list. These are my "Morganizing Methods." (Most of my clients like to use the term "Morganizing" and I encourage you to use it too!) These are the processes I work through when I work to reorganize any room. These methods work efficiently and effectively. If you follow them (all of them), you *will* work through your spaces and get things organized. Your rooms will look complete, and you will have systems that work. Yay! Commit to organizing in the ways that will work for you. Everything in these chapters will be guidelines for how to be organized. Then, *you* get to decide what your systems will look like and how detailed you make them.

An example of an organized space with systems. Each basket holds a different category, and no labels were required because of how visual it is. I added shelving to this closet in my laundry room to help with maximizing the space.

Morganizing Methods

Choose Your Priority Space

Start with one section, one drawer, one wall, one shelf. This is how progress is realized. Commit to getting one space in order (as much as possible) before moving on to the next. While there is a natural ripple effect and things do shift between spaces, avoid beginning projects in multiple rooms at the same time. When this happens it's easy to get stuck again because everything is churned up and things now feel ever more chaotic. Dominos is a fun game, but it's not a great way to organize! Keep your to-dos as singular tasks as much as possible. Work on the one thing (or space) in front of you. Consider the big picture but focus more so on each individual task.

Clear and Categorize

Clear everything out. Yes, everything (every single thing—don't take shortcuts). Adopt the mindset that *nothing is off-limits!* It is essential to touch everything to do a true assessment and get an accurate inventory check. This will help you to see what and how much you have of different items and categories. Believe me, it's usually more than you remember! I'll hear my clients say things like, *"That's where that went!"* or *"I didn't even know we had those."*

Create areas to sort your things into like piles. Use surfaces like a bed, table, or the floor. Spreading all your things out will give you a good perspective of your general categories. You can also begin to make piles that represent items that belong somewhere else (another space in your home, an item to return, donations, recycling, etc.). Leave them in their piles and don't start moving things to other locations until you have *everything* sorted. Don't start and stop and move from task to task. Your job is to pull it all out and put things together in like categories. Work in a wave. I usually start left to right or corner to corner. Avoid zig-zagging or skipping around. Think systematically and step by step. Top to bottom, side to side, and continue to tell yourself, *"like with like."*

Cull Like It's Your J-O-B

I was not familiar with the word "cull." However, over a few weeks I had numerous clients all use the word as we worked to declutter their belongings. Culling means getting rid of unwanted parts. Taking some items within a group and removing them. So yes, another way to describe decluttering. (I'm also going to make shirts that say, "Cull Time." Would you buy one?) Culling like it's your j-o-b is critical to getting your spaces organized.

As you work to pull everything out (see method number two), have garbage sacks, for either garbage collecting or to sack up the things you plan to donate. Be careful to designate what's what. Boxes and containers are also helpful because you can group items together. Touching things once equals more momentum. Looking over your piles and sections, be *ruthless* with what you will let go. I never suggest numbers or percentages. What you keep is up to you. However, stay focused on your big picture and consider the goal you have for your room or space. Then consider each item you touch through that filter.

Less is more. If you want your spaces to feel less cramped, then cull those belongings that are not adding to this feeling. This is the piece of the puzzle where if you can have a trusted friend or a loved one help you, it may be the accountability you need to help you move the needle.

Containment Is Key

Now that you have created categories, you need to contain things together to help organize. Every belonging in your home should have only one spot where it goes. All similar items need to be organized together. Gather any empty storage containers you have sitting around—bins, baskets, cubes. Have these pieces ready to work with you as you shift to creating your system(s). I'm a firm believer in using things you already have and repurposing items when they fit the need or space.

In the space you are working on, define the main purposes of the room. Then use containment to keep things grouped together. Your containers will help you segment and create boundaries. There are not specific numbers and rules to be concerned with here but consider your space and what it allows you to store. One client told me, *"I like to keep my 'extras' at the store, where they belong!"* You don't have to have massive amounts of backstock. And don't be afraid to think outside the box. Containers can be anything—a cupboard, a drawer, a bowl, a tray, a bin. You get the idea.

Create Labels Like a Boss

Labeling can help keep your systems working for you and your household. But not every space requires labels. The picture I shared previously of my laundry room closet is a great example of where labels were not necessarily required. Add them when it provides a benefit. Labels are helpful for those of us who are visual. They are also beneficial in spaces where you have multiple categories or want to have an inventory of what goes back in the storage container (i.e., which Christmas decor goes in which bin). I want my clients (and you!) to be able to send me to any place in their home and ask me to get them something. Then I want to be able to find it in a minute or two.

If a client sends me to her laundry room to get some glass cleaner and tells me to look for the bin labeled "cleaning supplies." You can bet that I would find it in under two minutes. Labeling makes it easier to find what you need and helps you (and others) know where to put things back (hopefully!). When you create a system with containment and add labels, you'll be more likely to avoid having to run to the store for something you already own and already have stored in your home.

Let's say your roommate asks you if you have an extra paint brush. Well, because you have organized systems in place, you would confidently answer, "Yes!" Then you would go and look in your box labeled "Paint Supplies." This is a *good enough* system that will save you time, money, and energy. All valuable things if you ask me!

A simple system like this is intuitive and easy to follow. Notice everything is labeled with inexpensive label tape. You can also use blue painter's tape or a chalk pen or printed labels—the sky's the limit when it comes to labeling. But keep it simple!

Curate and Cultivate

Curating an organized home is an ongoing process and will always be in flux. This isn't meant to discourage you; it's meant to empower you! Everything in life is ongoing. Organizing, like cleaning, decorating, and gardening, is an open-ended process. Once you get a space organized and have solid systems in place, you will then need to also make maintenance a priority. It's important to do daily, weekly, and monthly tidying to keep your systems healthy and functioning. This looks like resetting and being an intentional shopper, which we talked about in Chapter 5.

An organized space will only stay organized if it is curated and cultivated. It's the practice of putting things back where they belong. And trust me, this is often the hardest part. I'm a magician when it comes to getting my laundry in the washer and then to the dryer. I also do a pretty good job of getting everything folded and stacked in pretty piles. Nevertheless, I have the hardest time getting it all put away back into my closet. I do eventually force myself to do so because I know if I ignore it for too long then the snowball will only get bigger, and I want to avoid that at all costs!

Touching things once equals more momentum.

As you shift to the how-to, I suggest blocking off a set amount of time of two to four hours when you work on an organizing project. It takes a certain amount of time to get into the deeper work and realize progress. Turn off distractions, recruit help if that will be of benefit, and only work on the *one space* you've chosen. Getting organized is a messy process. Allow for the mess in the middle and celebrate when you get over the hump and you can get everything put away. It is the absolute best feeling!

I don't want to teach you how to organize like I do. I want to coach you how to organize in the ways that will work for you. I am not going to force you to make any choices or create habits that won't fit you. Your home needs to feel like it's yours and it's the nicest word you know. Are you ready? It's time to take back your home, one space at a time.

A corner in my parents' cozy and inviting living room.

Organize Your Spaces

This is a checklist for you to list out which rooms you want to address in your home. Use this to plan and track your progress. Remember, one section or space at a time.

Storing: _____

_____

Cooking: _____

_____

Living: _____

_____

Bathing: _____

_____

Clothing: _____

_____

Playing/Working: _____

_____

Sleeping: _____

_____

Chapter 8
Storing

"Your home is a living space,
not a storage space."

—Francine Jay

If you feel you need to reorganize every inch of your home, it can be challenging to know where to start. Let me help. Begin with your storage spaces: not off-sight storage units, the storage spaces in your home. I have discovered in my many years of professional organizing that this is often the best place to start. This could be your garage, a storage closet, an unfinished basement storage area, or your attic. Any place where you store things. The places where you put belongings that you don't use daily, which is why they are in storage.

I recommend you kick off organizing in a storage area, because then when you go to work in other spaces it is likely you'll find items that need to go in, you guessed it—storage! For example, down the road, when you are working to declutter your kitchen and find appliances you only use twice a year. You could then relocate them to a dedicated shelf in your storage closet, the one you already organized and has a dedicated shelf for, you guessed it—appliances!

Beginning in storage areas is not popular. I like to say it doesn't feel sexy. It's boring to go down to the dusty basement or deal with cluttered piles in an overcrowded garage. But trust me, getting this done first can help the entire home organizing process.

This is my car loaded with matching and coordinated bins for a storage space. If you are starting "fresh" with your storage space, invest in products that will stack and nest together (same brand and style). This will help take better advantage of your space and will look nice too!

Choose one section of storage to work on and make this your foundation. If you've felt stuck with where to start with getting organized, now you know! Refer to the "Morganizing Methods" and work through them, one step at a time. The good news is you've already checked off the first step, so you are off to a great start!

> According to the Self-Storage Association, a trade group, around 11 percent of US households have a self-storage unit.[5] Now, if you happen to have a storage unit, this is more than fine. You are getting zero judgment from me. In fact, we rented a storage space for a short season when our daughter moved abroad. We needed a place to put her belongings while she was gone, and for us, this worked. There are definite reasons and seasons for when a storage unit can be a lifesaver. I would never encourage or discourage someone from having a storage unit. The only question I would ask is, *"Why do you have one?"*
>
> Remember to always ask *why* first. It's a great place to start and will help you to better evaluate your priorities. If you have a storage unit, consider if that commitment aligns with your organizing goals and what you want to experience within your home and life. Is it benefiting you or costing you? (And not just monetarily, but emotionally, mentally, or physically?) If you make a choice to part with your storage unit, I recommend only decluttering and editing things in the unit *after* you've addressed your entire home organization. If you do things in this order, you will have a better idea of what space you have available in your home (or don't have). If you've done a good job culling and your home is more streamlined, you will likely have more space available. Either way, it will give you a good perspective for when you go to sort through the storage unit. You will have a clear understanding of what can be relocated back to your home and what you need to donate, sell, or recycle.

---

5   White, Martha C, "Americans Went All-In on Self Storage," New York Times, Nytimes.com, www.nytimes.com/2024/04/26/business/self-storage-business.html.

This is a snapshot of the shelves we use in our basement storage area. All the bins maximize the space and are labeled for easy recall.

Homes

After you have gotten everything out and edited, ask how this storage space needs to function for you and the others who use the space. Is this a garage shelving unit that needs to house your family's outdoor and camping supplies? Does this closet need to store all your hobby and craft supplies? Or is this a basement storage room where you want to put all holiday decor and personal keepsakes? Start macro with the larger umbrella categories (sports, holidays, toys, gifts). Then go micro, into zones.

When we don't define a storage area they can all too quickly and easily become "catch-all" spots. You know what a catch-all spot is good for? Nothing. Spots like these become chaotic and continue to catch more and more as time marches on. If we don't have an easy-to-follow organizing system in our garages, then who's going to put anything back where it belongs? If it doesn't belong anywhere specifically, you can guarantee it won't be put back anywhere specifically. Be precise with what is located where. The foundation of home organization is creating homes!

These shelves house several different zones of our household and outdoor things. Using clear bins is another great tool for those who do better with more visibility.

Zones

I learned the term "zoning" when I worked for Target. One of the jobs at the end of my shift was to zone certain sections of the store. Each team member was assigned an area and instructed to put everything back in its home. This helped clean up the shopping activity and prepare the store so shoppers the next day could *find what they are looking for*! (My number one goal for being organized.)

When someone tells me they struggle with organizing, I get it. I think they are also saying they find zoning exhausting. It is. You must walk to and from. Picking up, sorting, carrying, and putting things back. It takes time, energy, and attention, and can also feel like tedious work.

Consider this: what would our shopping experiences look like if there was no method to the madness? What if all the fresh green produce was mixed haphazardly in with the socks and underwear? Or all the varieties of rice and pasta were casually spread throughout the store in multiple locations? How would you ever find the Thai Orchid Jasmine Rice you need to buy for the new recipe you want to try? If there was no order in retail stores, I wonder if these businesses would even survive! Shoppers would feel stressed and overwhelmed trying to find the items on their shopping lists. It would feel more like a wild goose chase than a casual stroll through clean and organized aisles—Starbucks drink in your hand.

Zoning is critical. Once you've defined your storage space and spelled out the homes. Now get in the zone! This looks like breaking things down more where it is required. The photo on the previous page shows our other shelves in our garage. I purchased bins that fully filled the shelves and then zoned everything into smaller categories. This created a micro system within a macro one and uses boundaries. (Boundaries are good!) All the yard stuff is stored together, swim things are combined into two bins, and even the pets have a bin for their extra supplies, those items that aren't used as frequently. Creating zones will result in longer-term solutions for your systems. When you add containment, it gives you a natural boundary of how much you can keep of each category. For example, if I bring home more swimming supplies, if they cannot be added to one of the two bins I already have designated "swim," then I will need to cull something. Make this a practice. If new items cannot fit, then inventory levels need to be readdressed.

These shelves are the "homes" for David's and my shoes. We keep most of our pairs of shoes here and then dressier shoes or seasonal shoes are upstairs in our closet. This is a clear and specific use of these shelves.

Best Storage Organizing Products

- Matching bins (same style/brand) are helpful; they stack easier and will make things look more cohesive.

- Shelves that are the right size to store containers; maximize space and fill it up. (Measure twice, buy once.)

- Any storage system that will take advantage of your walls or ceilings—go vertical.

Chapter 9
Cooking

"Happiness is a small house, but with a big kitchen."

—Alfred Hitchcock

The heart of the home is often the kitchen. It's where everyone congregates, and lasting memories are made. When my kids were toddlers, they would do noisy parades around the kitchen island (which of course made me smile as I tried to maneuver around them to get dishes loaded into the dishwasher). When guests come over, they immediately find their way to our kitchen, and it is where they choose to gather. They either lean against the counters or find a seat. There is something about cooking and eating that naturally brings people together. Dining and feasting are ways for us to connect, celebrate, and make lasting memories.

If I had to tally up the hours I've spent in my kitchen—cooking, cleaning, and organizing—I don't think I could count that high! Raising three kids (now all adults) and handling the meal prepping for many of those years kept me in the kitchen daily. And thankfully for the most part I loved it!

Wherever you are with cooking (love it or dread it), my guess is that either you or those you live with must do some form of meal prepping. I mean, we all must eat, right? Now, if you don't need to cook much or your kitchen is already simplistic, you can move on to another chapter. But if you are on the other end of the continuum and want to be the next Master Chef, then take a seat at the counter. We're going to open the cupboards, pull out the drawers, look in the fridge, and have a heart-to-heart.

Whether you have a small kitchen or a large kitchen, your approach to how you organize it is the same. I will show you different spaces and guide you through your kitchen and dining organization by keeping things simple. Work to avoid feeling discouraged! If you feel short on space or if your kitchen is outdated or if you'll feel extremely overwhelmed with all that is shoved in your cupboards, that is okay!

Embrace your space and let's make it work for you today.

A great example of a basic pantry space organized. My client Kendra maximizes the space by keeping her inventory levels in check and using containment where it provides her benefit.

When you commit to following my methods (outlined in Part 3) and begin to organize your kitchen one section at a time, you *will* find more space! If you have not done a full declutter of your kitchen in the last five years, you will need to touch each one of your items. However, if you do regular resets—seasonally or annually—you may not need to pull out all your items. You get to decide but be honest with yourself! Doing an overall reorganization can be a huge step for your kitchen, helping to make it function even better for you and your loved ones or roommates.

If things have been tucked away and are out of sight and out of mind, do the tough work and get it all exposed. Revealing the issues will help you to address them! Also, make sure to move into other connected eating and dining areas. If you have a breakfast nook or a formal dining room, make a point to look at those spaces too. Determine if everything you are storing in there is still needed and used. Ask yourself if what you are keeping *is* what you are using.

In our current house, we have a well-lit and spacious pantry. I could still over-stuff it and fill it, but I don't. The bins work well to create division and I don't label them because our preferences change constantly!

Eating

An important question to ask is how often you need to or want to cook and prepare food. Let's face it—many of us (I'm halfway raising my hand) would be more than okay going out to eat more often or getting takeout on the regular! While I enjoy parts of cooking, I really do! I would like it even more if it didn't require all the other parts: shopping, prepping, and cleaning up. It can be a big ordeal.

Nonetheless, I do want to eat healthier and stay within our food budget, so we choose to cook many of our meals at home. This means we use our air fryer, blender, coffee maker, and mixer consistently. Most of our appliances are well-loved and we use them regularly. This should be the goal for you too. If you cook more at home than not, then have the appliances and equipment pieces that will help you to prepare your meals. Whereas if you don't cook much at home, you can likely streamline your essentials to only what you use. If I had a dollar for every Instant Pot I've taken for donation, I'd be a rich woman. (I'm kidding, but I have donated a lot of them!) Nothing against the Instant Pot but avoid buying the latest and greatest appliance just because it's all the rave.

Preparing

Next, ask yourself if you fall more into the category of being a cook or baker. This is important to identify, because if you lean more toward one style of preparing food over another then you can likely adjust how many items and/or appliances you have. I have had several clients who are into grilling and therefore have nice-sized stashes of grilling seasonings and fancy barbeque tools. They actively use these items to cook and grill and therefore keeping real estate open for these tools is a priority for them. Other clients love to bake and so for them it is important to create space for storing their cake-decorating supplies and cookie cutters. And if you are both a cook and a baker, that's fine too. Make space available for what you use regularly and what is most important to you. If you have specialty items or things that are seldom used, consider relocating them to an extra closet or storage area. Don't be afraid to think outside of the box. Not everything "kitchen" has to be in the kitchen. It is your home; do what works for you in every drawer, shelf, and cupboard.

My clients like to bake a lot and therefore need an organized system in their cupboard. Aesthetics and clear labels were also important to them. (Always honor your preferences!)

Working

I've had many clients tell me that when they moved into their house, they put things away without any rhyme or reason, which is understandable. Moving is exhausting and it can be hard to do deeper organizing work when you just want to get things unpacked and put away. However, you want to avoid this now that you are working to streamline and create structure in your spaces. When working to establish an effective system in your kitchen, put things away with attention and intention. Without order, it will make it harder for you to keep your kitchen organized.

To set your kitchen up for long-term success, consider the kitchen "work" triangle. This is defined as *"a concept used to determine efficient kitchen layouts that are both aesthetically pleasing and functional. The primary tasks in a home kitchen are carried out between the cook top, the sink, and the refrigerator. These three points and the imaginary lines between them make up what kitchen experts call the work triangle. The idea is that when these three elements are close (but not too close) to one another, the kitchen will be easy and efficient to use, cutting down on wasted steps."*[6]

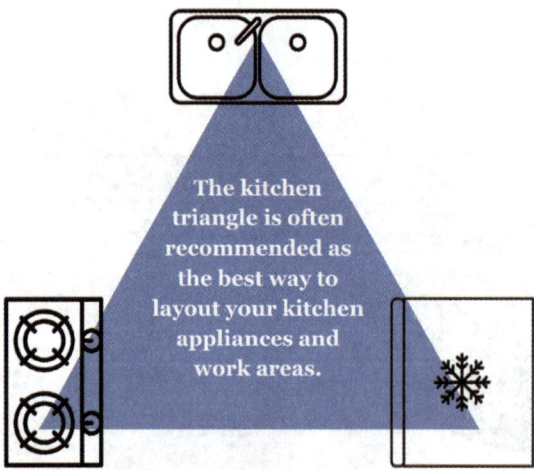

---

6   Kitchen Work Triangle, Wikipedia, March 30, 2024, en.wikipedia.org/wiki/Kitchen_work_triangle.

Think through where you work in your kitchen. What tasks do you take care of on the island? Where do you do most of your food prep? Which counter do you put items on when you pull them out of the refrigerator? Where do dirty dishes land or dishes that need to be air dried? You likely already have some patterns so think through what's working and what's not. Celebrate what's working and then work to change what needs adjusting.

This was a client's pantry we worked to reorganize. It's a great space, but by dialing in the "systems" we were able to make it more functional for their everyday needs.

Arranging

After you have taken everything out, categorized, and culled the items you no longer need, determine the containers you want to have in your kitchen (Morganizing Method number four). Assigning homes for your items and then zoning things together will create solid systems. If you haven't yet looked at Chapter 8, you might find it helpful to flip back there for more how-to on setting up homes and zones. Then, make a list if you need to shop for additional supplies. Certain products can help with storing and segmenting your kitchen items. While not all organizing supplies add to a space, some do! Check out my lists at the end of each chapter for the types of products I recommend for different rooms.

If you have previous locations and systems where things have worked well, then put those things back into those spaces. The process of reorganizing is to continually think through what the flow and function of your kitchen needs to be. As you put things into groupings and sections, keep asking yourself, *"Where should this go?"*

Let's say you love to make pasta, then you will want to have dedicated shelving to hold your different pastas, noodles, and sauces. I wouldn't put these items out of reach in the back of a deep cupboard. Or if you cook breakfast every day, then your espresso machine, blender, and waffle maker might need to all be within easy reach. Consider also where you do most of your prep work. For example, strainers should be near your sink for easy access. Put knives and cutting boards close to each other so the task can be easily started (and near the sink might be helpful too). Designate a cupboard (or two) for the appliances you don't prefer to leave on your counter. Avoid having things not grouped and keep things closer in reach to you that you use more frequently. Your harder-to-reach and higher places are perfect spots for seldom-used items like vases or holiday dishes. Also, only move things from their original packaging into storage containers if you prefer this and if you can keep up with the regular maintenance. I don't generally recommend this as a system, unless it is a fit for you. I know you have seen beautiful pictures of perfectly zoned containers of food. All unpackaged and sitting pretty on the shelves. While yes, it is pretty, it is also a lot to keep up with. Most food items already come in storage containers, and you keep things simpler for yourself by not creating more steps. (Unless this step is important to you!) Then, once you have everything in order, make a point to give a kitchen tour to everyone else in your home. Systems are followed when systems are understood.

This is my setup of my spices. I encourage you not to be too spicy! (See below for more on this.)

Spice Organization

I've discovered most people have a spice problem. Yes, they are too spicy! No, what I mean is that most of us overly load up on spices. I was determined to get to the bottom of this spice overconsumption! I researched the most common spices one should have on hand, and I came up with this list of twenty-four. It is below for your easy reference. This is not an exhaustive list and depending on how often you cook and/or your preferences around cooking, this list may serve you well or you may need to add or subtract. Either way, work to pare down and keep the essentials on hand.

My favorite way to organize spices is in uniform containers with matching labels (see my spices below). Then you can either use drawer inserts, turntables, or a tiered shelf to help visually see all of them immediately. Paring down your spices and making your system uniform will make it easier for you to find a spice when you need it to cook with it.

Spices

Spice	Purchase Date	Expiration Date
[ ] Basil		
[ ] Bay Leaves		
[ ] Cayenne		
[ ] Cinnamon		
[ ] Chili Powder		
[ ] Cloves		
[ ] Coriander		
[ ] Cream of Tarter		
[ ] Cumin		
[ ] Curry		
[ ] Dill		
[ ] Garlic (Powder/Salt)		
[ ] Ginger		
[ ] Mustard Powder		
[ ] Nutmeg		
[ ] Oregano		
[ ] Paprika		
[ ] Parsley		
[ ] Pepper		
[ ] Rosemary		
[ ] Sage		
[ ] Salt		
[ ] Turmeric		
[ ] Thyme		
[ ]		
[ ]		
[ ]		
[ ]		
[ ]		

MM

Many grocery stores (like Sprouts) have bulk spices you can purchase to restock your spice jars at home. This is a great way to be sustainable and keep your spices organized.

Best Kitchen Organizing Products

- Drawer dividers, trays, or tension rods help to segment things like silverware, utensils, and towels.

- Small and medium-sized bins/baskets help to corral like categories (water bottle lids, cookie cutters, appliance parts, or backstock spices).

- Turntables help to make a tight or deep corner more reachable and accessible.

- Large baskets/bins for bigger bulk items: use these on the floor of a pantry or up high on a shelf to maximize vertical storage space.

- An inset drawer knife holder gets more things off your counter and helps to decrease clutter.

- A "junk drawer" insert organizer—yes, you can have a junk drawer—but you must organize it!

- Pretty holder for fruit—a bowl, basket, or tray.

- Pan and/or lid holder will help to more easily stack and organize your pans and lids.

Chapter 10
Living

"We are always getting ready
to live but never living."

—Ralph Waldo Emerson

Life is passing us all by, whether we like it or not. David and I will be empty nesters in a few short months and there is nothing we can do to change this fact. Time keeps marching on! For the first time in what seems like forever, it will be just the two of us. It is bittersweet. I look at my now adult children and can still see their sweet young faces looking back at me. The last twenty-four years have given us so many beautiful and precious memories.

Other parents will ask me if it is hard for me to let my kids move on. I usually answer, *"Yes and no."* Seeing my kids spread their wings and soar helps me to more easily let them fly away. It is sad, but it is also happy to watch them grow into who they are meant to be. It makes me incredibly happy to see them living their lives to the fullest. It is what I have always hoped and prayed for them to experience. I wholeheartedly believe our lives are meant to be lived!

Much of our time at home is spent in our living spaces. So, as we turn to this next space, choose a room where you "live." This could be a great room, family room, den—you pick. It's a broad category and I encourage you to choose a space where you want to live more comfortably and simply. Living spaces often meet our needs for relaxing, socializing, communicating, entertaining, and more. After selecting your room, then take the next steps. Your steps will always start by working through the six Morganizing Methods (Part 3). If you need to refresh your memory, please go back and reread the steps. Then commit to redefining your room so you can live well and embrace all that your living space can offer.

Live Comfortably

Begin by defining what a comfortable space feels like for you. What layers could you add to create more coziness? Are there things you need to remove that aren't adding value to your room? Where do people naturally find themselves resting and settling in? How can you dial up comfortability and the sense of welcome?

I love touches of candles and blankets—think *hygge*. *Hygge* (a Danish word) references feelings of coziness. Ways to make you and others feel most comfortable and at home. In warmer months this could look like outdoor lighting or adding soft pillows to your patio furniture. Think of someone's home where you've felt incredibly at ease. What about their home made you feel that way? You don't need to recreate the wheel. Do what you have seen works! Use inspiration to motivate you and then design your areas to reflect your preferences and tastes. Comfortable for you may not look the same to someone else, but you know what makes you feel cozy and relaxed.

Live Simply

Clarify how your living space needs to meet your needs. What do you want and/or need to do in this space? Do you have regular movie nights, and would a big couch and dim lighting add to the experience? Or are game nights more your jam? Would adding a storage piece, like a console or bookshelf, be a strategic way to store your games and puzzles in one spot? Maybe you want a corner of your room dedicated to music and instruments. Then specify a spot for your guitars to hang vertically and a place for your keyboard to stay plugged in. Adding baskets to hold music books will also help with organizing the needs of the room.

However you choose to characterize your living space, choose simplicity. Take out the excess. Living simply requires less. Return things that don't belong to the spots in your home where they do belong. Try to only designate three functions for the room, not more. Avoid setting up a "choose your own adventure" type of space. Minimize choices and distractions where you can. Let it be an area that clearly tells you what to do when you arrive and where you can settle in easily.

Live Well

Living spaces can quickly become rooms where too many things take place. One example of this may be that someone is working from home in the family room or den. Are there times when this is fine? Yes. However, I would encourage you or whoever works from home to set up a specific spot for work. It is harder to relax and unwind if your work is piled up in front of you or if you can see your computer monitor staring back at you. If you need to redefine your living space as a workspace, then do so and be clear about the purpose of the room. In this case, your living space might be less of a place to relax and more of a room where you can focus and do your productive work. Try not to overlap too many purposes for a room. If you need to have a workspace within a living space, try to incorporate some form of division. Use an armoire, room divider, or curtain—something you can close at the end of your work time. Allowing you to shift the room from a place of production to a space for restoration. Without clear boundaries it is easy for things to unravel and feel increasingly chaotic.

When it comes to your living space(s), maybe you would like more available space or wish you could redecorate everything from floor to ceiling. However, if you can't make these kinds of changes today, that is okay! You *can* design your room with what you have available. Clear out as much as you can to create more breathing room. This alone will give a facelift to any space. Then only add back the important pieces. Those items that fall under your umbrella of the "homes" for your room (strive for a maximum of three!). Your homes could be reading, watching TV, and socializing. Or any combination. But be specific. Specificity helps to create solid systems.

Design your living space with intention and purpose. Allow your eyes to rest by not putting too much into the space. Allow room to live. Most importantly, make your space *yours*! Living well means choosing to make your space work for you for today. Your living spaces should be a place of comfort, connection, and whatever else is important to you. Live well.

Best Living Room Organizing Products

- Remote controllers need a spot, a basket, bin, drawer, or tray.

- A coat rack for guests says hello and please stay awhile.

- Shoes-off house? Have a basket or tray for guests when they arrive.

- Slippers by the front door for guests or housemates say, "Get comfy!"

- Designate a small table for a drop zone, a place to set keys, phones, etc.

- Baskets are your friends; use them to group blankets, toys, magazines, books.

- Utilize a console, dresser, or armoire to help corral belongings. Doors and drawers help keep things stored and out of sight.

- Incorporate multipurpose pieces of furniture that also provide you with storage (i.e., an ottoman with storage or a coffee table with drawers).

Chapter 11
Bathing

"Rest and self-care are so important. When you take time to replenish your spirit, it allows you to serve others from the overflow. You cannot serve from an empty vessel."

—Eleanor Brownn

Please tell me I'm not the only one guilty of thinking a new beauty product will change my life. I will be at the store and see a new dry shampoo product claiming to work wonders or a face lotion that promises to erase fine lines. My hand will reach out in what feels like autopilot and toss them into my cart without thinking. It's as if the marketers know me by name and know what exactly will persuade me to put something in my shopping cart. I mentioned earlier that I pressed "add to cart" via a TikTok ad for a neck cream that came with rave reviews. I am surprisingly happy with it, but hands down, it has not changed my life!

There is a high demand for beauty products, and I am right there pushing to be at the front of the line. As a society we are hyper-focused on looking younger. We want products to help us reverse all signs of aging. Our choices are endless, and the influencer marketing is effective.

Now, I'm not saying you need to become a minimalist and pare down to only six beauty products. Absolutely not! It's fine to prioritize those products that make you look and feel great. Taking care of yourself is something I will always support and encourage. In fact, we often err on the other side. We all too easily push self-care to the bottom of our to-do lists. Listing them as suggestions or almost optional activities. Something we will try to get to if or when we have time. I think self-care should stay at the top of our to-do lists. Taking care of ourselves should be one of our highest and most protected priorities. When we nurture our needs, it then allows us to show up and be more present.

When we nurture our needs, it then allows us to show up and be more present.

As we turn to your bathing space(s)—your primary bathroom, maybe a powder room—I'll even give you the latitude of applying this chapter to any type of cleaning space in your home. After all, cleaning and bathing are both things that provide us with a reset, either to us or to our spaces. These two categories also share a lot of similarities so there is a natural tie in. Everything about my approach to organizing is organic, and this chapter is no exception.

For some of you, a bathroom may be a relatively easy space to reorganize. Maybe you don't wear any makeup, or you have used the same type of shampoo and conditioner for the past four decades. Perhaps you prefer to spend no more than five minutes in the morning getting ready. So, if this is you and your space is already in the zone, you know what I'll say. *Move on.*

The rest of you: Get ready. We're going to look in the mirror and evaluate which organizing systems are working and which are not. It's time to open your medicine cabinet, look at your linen closet, and open that bathroom drawer (you know, the one that barely opens because it is so overstuffed). We will dive into the art of editing all things bathing and cleaning!

Practical

Schedule enough time to work on this section of your home and be realistic. When a room is smaller, we can assume it won't take us as long to pull everything out and edit. However, a smaller space can often take the same amount of time, if not more. Especially if there are lots of smaller items. (Nail polish bottles and bobby pins, I'm looking at you!) You will work through the same methods we have in your other spaces and what I want you to think about as you examine your products is this, make a commitment to stick with what works. Let me elaborate.

This is a simple system. I only need to stock these every few months (or more). It is pretty and practical all in one.

When I started wearing mascara in middle school—something I still wear to this day—I followed in my mom's footsteps; I picked up the green and pink tube made by Maybelline at my local drugstore. This is the same mascara my mom used, and she recommended it to me. Well, it has never let me down and requires zero decision-making. My favorite kind of decision to make! I pick it up on repeat; it's my go-to. From time to time, however, I have been swayed to try a different brand. Usually, one that promises me that my eyelashes will double in thickness (yes, please!). Then when I try this new *miracle* mascara I'm underwhelmed. It feels lumpy, my lashes stick together, and the shape of the wand feels awkward. So, what do I do? I reach for my green and pink mascara and life returns to normal and easy.

Make a commitment to stick with what works.

It's all too common to want to try the latest and greatest. Sometimes it may be worth it, but in many cases, the saying *"If it's not broke, don't fix it!"* applies. If you have specific items that have never let you down and they are your go-to items, I encourage you to keep going to them. Avoid spending time and energy sourcing and shopping for something new (to you) that may in fact not be *any* better! Or if you want to try something new, make a point to use your original item(s) first. This way you are actively practicing the art of bringing in one thing and taking one thing out, something you should always practice. When we treat our front door as a revolving door it helps to keep our clutter minimized instead of maximized.

Pretty

Your bathroom spaces can be both practical *and* pretty. The key is to narrow down what you use and love. Think through your morning and evening routines and ensure you have the supplies on hand that match what you emphasize and prioritize. It's easy to overstuff our cabinets because we tell ourselves we use (or will use) all the things we have purchased, when in actuality we only use a small percentage of the products.

Say you like having face masks on hand, but when it comes down to it, you don't make time to use them. The question to ask yourself is, "Why do I have a huge stack of face masks? Why do I have these and buy them if I don't use them?" It's better to admit this than to continue accumulating and adding to your inventory. Perhaps your new guideline for yourself could be not to buy any more face masks. Instead, you could schedule a facial for yourself a few times a year. You could use that appointment as a form of self-care. The result would be less clutter in your bathroom and you would get to enjoy a spa facial.

Organizing is all about choices. Choose well regarding what you need and use daily. Specify what goes where and pare down where you can. If you are intentional with how much inventory you store, you will be able to better maintain your bathing spaces. Use your shopping lists and stick with the products that work best for you. This applies to cleaning products too. Don't be enticed by the newest polish, scrub, or mop that says it will work wonders. You know what works wonders? Picking up the polish and using it. Scrubbing the sponge as it is intended to be used. Or picking up the mop to clean your floors! Don't be guilty of stocking up on things you will not make the time to use. Everything that takes up real estate should be of value to you. And everything of value should be given adequate real estate.

Best Bathroom Organizing Products

- Drawer liners and/or trays are essential to keeping messes contained from products like toothpaste or makeup.

- Turntables help with accessibility and categorizing.

- Storage containers on your counters can be both practical and pretty ways to store everyday products (like cotton balls or Q-Tips).

- Use baskets or containers to store bathing and/or cleaning items in your backstock area.

- Go vertical: hang up your hair dryer, ironing board, or jewelry.

- Trays or small bins help to corral those items that habitually stay on your counters (which is more than okay).

Chapter 12

Clothing

"Stress doesn't really go with my outfit."

—Unknown

Design fatigue is a challenge especially when it comes to deciding what to wear. But I don't want you wasting your time and energy getting dressed! I hope choosing what you will wear each day is one of the easiest decisions you have to make. So, how do you make this a reality?

To get your clothing areas reorganized, identify several aspects of your wardrobe and create a plan for your closet. Start by thinking through your personal style, what colors look best on you, and defining how you want to dress for your age and body. Then consider what your lifestyle demands from you and how you need to dress for your day-to-day living. Lastly, consider if creating a capsule wardrobe may be of benefit. You don't have to create a capsule wardrobe, but I'll explain the benefits of why simplifying your style and paring down your number of clothing pieces can create more outfits for you.

Like every space in your home, you will work through my methods step by step. As you pull everything out and edit, also make time to try things on. I know it's a pain, but it will help you to make better choices. Being discerning with what will stay and what will go from your wardrobe is easier when you try on the pants that don't fit right or the shirt that has those annoying sleeves. Trying things on helps you to know why you are or aren't wearing certain pieces. You will feel the fit (good or bad) and see that the hem is either too long or too short.

Depending on how big your wardrobe is will determine how much time you need to set aside for this organizing task. Be honest with how many items you need to process and think through which sections would work well to break down the size of the task. Also address your accessories—jewelry, seasonal clothing, any items that tie into your overall wardrobe. If you are overwhelmed, I see you. It can be tough to dig into all the pieces of your wardrobe, but it is so freeing when you are done. After resetting everything, you will have a more stylized and systemized closet. One that will make it easier for you to get dressed. Everything you hang back up or fold and put away will be the pieces you wear *and* love. Doesn't that sound amazing? Let's take back your closet and eliminate the stress of getting dressed!

Let's take back your closet and eliminate the stress of getting dressed!

Styles and Colors

Begin by examining your fashion style. Here are some examples to choose from. Look these over and see which one(s) you think best describes your style. You are likely a combination of one or two (or more). This list is by no means all-inclusive; it's a framework for you to work from. If none of these speak to you, create your own! Determining your style is step one to a better-organized closet. Most of us gravitate toward a specific style of some sort. Naming this and acknowledging it will help you to build an even better inventory of clothes.

- Casual—relaxed, comfort
- Classic—elegant, timeliness
- Bohemian—natural, artistic
- Chic—trendy, timeliness
- Sporty—athletic, laid-back
- Preppy—coordinated, conservative
- Minimalist—neutrals, simple
- Formal—tailored, professional

Next, think through which colors look best on you. You can do this by looking through photos of yourself in different outfits and noticing which colors look better on you. Which tones highlight your skin tone? What colors make your eyes pop? Are there hues that make you look more washed out or tired? Take note! There are some great books and resources out there as well where you can get more information on color styling. I was recently given a color analysis by my sister as a gift. It was helpful to see the colors I should wear more of and learn that if I'm wearing a black top, I should put something lighter near my face. A scarf or cardigan will help to lighten the darker color and look better with my skin tone. Small shifts like this can make a big difference in how clothes look on you.

Consider also which types of clothing you prefer to wear and which cuts fit you the best. Are you tall or petite? Long-waisted or short-waisted? Do you want to downplay certain features? Knowing what looks best on you will help you to purchase clothing pieces that accentuate you positively. Avoid continuing to purchase clothes you won't wear because you don't like the way they fit or feel. Also give thought to your age and life season. When you continue dressing as you did twenty years ago you might find you are stuck in a rut. To know what fit you prefer, always try on clothes before buying them. Or if you order things online, make yourself try them on when they arrive. (And return what doesn't work to help cut down on clutter!) Making intentional choices on the front end will save you time, money, and energy.

Lifestyle

I don't dress up to go to the office. Instead, I need workout clothes for teaching fitness classes, outfits that work for my day-to-day home and life management, and clothes that facilitate my ability to do my organizing work with my clients in their homes and businesses. I am less concerned with being fashionable and more focused on my clothing being both functional and comfortable.

To narrow down which types of clothes I want and need to wear, I have defined three category styles for myself and my closet. They are sporty, casual, and minimalist. These are the outfits I need in my closet for my daily living and working. Knowing what my needs are and how I like to dress helped me to better evaluate the types of clothing pieces I should invest in and which items I should eliminate altogether from my closet.

Likewise, I want you to come up with styles and categories of clothing you need to have in your wardrobe. Think through your regular activities and define your overarching themes and needs. This can then be used to help you set up your closet in "like" sections. I place all my athletic clothes in one area, all my Morganize with Me branded clothing and black bottoms together, and my daily uniform of jeans or shorts are all in a spot. This approach to setting up my closet makes getting dressed for me a breeze!

Another detail to contemplate is if your wardrobe fits with where you live. Sometimes if you have moved from one place to another, you may be holding on to clothes that are now not as necessary in your new location. This could be because of a different climate, culture, or even a change in role. Avoid the tendency to hold on to the past; instead choose to live in the present! If you now live in a beach town that is sunny and warm year-round, you don't necessarily need to keep all your winter sweaters. Consider holding on to the ones you love and designating them to a seasonal section for when you travel or vacation. You don't need to get rid of everything from a past role or previous location but be thoughtful with how much you hold on to from a former location.

Capsule Wardrobe

Wouldn't it be great to only have complimenting and coordinating outfits? Do you love the idea of never again having to say, *"I have nothing to wear!"* If this rings true to you, then a capsule wardrobe may be just what you need to create. What is it you ask? *"Susie Faux, revived the term in the 1970s. According to Faux, a capsule wardrobe is a collection of a few essential items of clothing that do not go out of fashion such as skirts, trousers, and coats, which can then be augmented with seasonal pieces."*[7]

If you want to go in this direction, take a relaxed approach. A capsule wardrobe focuses on minimizing the number of clothing pieces in your wardrobe to then maximize your number of outfits. It is less important to focus on the exact number of clothing pieces, and instead highlight what a streamlined closet would look like for you.

Here are a few foundational principles that will help you in setting up a simplified capsule wardrobe. This is my list of tools I have implemented to help me pare down my pieces. As a result, I now have fewer pieces yet more outfits! Don't overthink a capsule wardrobe. Instead think of the categories of clothing you need, the seasons you dress for, and how you want your closet

---

7   Capsule Wardrobe, Wikipedia, March 29, 2024, en.wikipedia.org/wiki/Capsule_wardrobe.

to look and feel. Every piece of clothing you keep in your wardrobe should make you *and* your closet look better!

Capsule Wardrobe Tips

- **Life:** Evaluate your style, lifestyle, and location.
- **Basics:** Invest in quality classic (neutral) pieces.
- **Comfort:** Dress for form and function before fashion.
- **Turnover:** Schedule a periodic inventory (decluttering) of your wardrobe.
- **Outfits:** Every piece of clothing in your closet should have a partner.
- **Plan:** Shop for new clothing (only) from a specific list.
- **Bling:** Accessories are your number one accessory.

It is all too easy to stay in a pattern of mindless shopping or casual online ordering. When we continue to unintentionally overbuy clothing, our drawers and closet rods will remain overstuffed. This is then when decision fatigue sets in. Only buy what you wear *and* love. Love it or leave it.

My client Shelly keeps a section of her tops on her lower clothing rod because these are her go-to items and they are easier for her to reach on the lower rod. These are the shirts she loves to wear and seeing them grouped helps her to get dressed more easily. Setting up things in sections helps to categorize and guide your outfit selections.

Best Closet Organizing Products

- Match your hangers. Any style can work well. When they coordinate, it will instantly uplevel your closet.

- Use all your available vertical hanging space. There are lots of ways to use walls and high shelves to help store things. Don't waste space!

- Install wall hooks to hold frequently used items like tank tops, bathrobes, sweatshirts, or clothing items you will wear one more time before washing.

- Clear or solid bins/baskets help to hold select categories (hats, swimsuits, gloves, and more).

- Designate laundry baskets for however you do your laundry (darks/lights, athletic/dressy). Make laundry collection easy.

- Drawer dividers help create separation in larger drawers.

- Set a box or bag in your closet area to collect clothes that you want to donate. Anytime you try something on that doesn't "work" anymore, put it in the donation spot. Make easy decisions easy to make!

Chapter 13
Playing/Working

"Focus on being productive
instead of busy."

—Tim Ferriss

We need to have places for both working and playing in our homes. Both activities generally require adequate space and will also benefit from organized systems. I'm going to touch on these two spaces in this chapter as they are both similar yet different. Workspaces lean toward any form of production. This could be a craft, hobby, or a job: anything you work on that requires space and quiet to focus. A play space will gravitate toward entertainment and/or recreation. Again, define and decide which space(s) these may be for you in your home. (And maybe they don't apply to you, which is more than fine!)

This chapter will help you to organize and prioritize the systems you need to make your work and play spaces increasingly functional. When we intentionally design our spaces to meet our needs, it will feel less defeating to walk into the space. Instead, the room will rise to meet us and our needs. Doesn't that sound like a win-win?

> **When we intentionally design our spaces to meet our needs, it feels less defeating to walk into the space.**

Play Zone

Now, I'll talk specifically about playrooms because this is a common area where homeowners want help. Toys are overrunning my clients' homes, and they call me in desperation to help calm the chaos! If a playroom for children doesn't directly relate to you, consider a playroom to be any recreational space. Maybe you have a home gym, sports area, or room with a pool table and wet bar. You can still apply the tools for a playroom in these spaces. And if you don't have a playroom of any kind then maybe you need to establish one! It's good to have space(s) where you can invest in some form of recreation. My current spaces like this in our home are our home gym and hot tub. Although, if I'm being honest, I don't spend much time in our home gym, just the hot tub. Who can blame me?

I love when I get to help reorganize a playroom. It can be such a fun space to help reclaim. I also enjoy getting to step back into my younger years when I was raising my babies. However, let me be clear. Reorganizing a playroom is usually not easy! When I go to work in a space like this, my clients (the parents) are often overwhelmed by the massive number of toys scattered everywhere. And their children are inundated with how many toys they can choose from. Now, let me clarify again, I don't believe in strict rules (or any rules, for that matter) for how many toys one should have. It's not that simple. Paring down to a specific number of toys is not a formula or an exact science. Begin with defining how you want the area you've dedicated for your kids to play in to look, feel, and function. Start here.

For some floor plans, having one defined room for all toys works well. For other homes, it may be better to have the toys in your children's individual or shared bedrooms. Or perhaps a combination of two or more spaces? This is your decision to make but do try to minimize the total number of places toys live. When things get spread out, that's when clutter usually increases and often exponentially! Once you have designated where the toys will live, then you need to determine your capacity for how many toys you will keep in your space(s). I know there are layers with toys, like all belongings, but sometimes there are even more layers to peel back with with toys. Many are gifts, hand-me-downs, or items your child isn't ready to part with. There is a place to be sensitive and thoughtful, but you can also guide them through the process and also be honest with yourself. Are you holding on to some of the toys because of nostalgia or not wanting the season to end? Keep in mind, some editing may be done with your children assisting you and some may be better done without them.

I loved designing and organizing this space for a cute family. These IKEA shelves and bins do a great job of keeping the toy clutter contained and stylized.

I suggest to my clients that when there are items you or your child are unsure about holding on to, consider boxing them up and labeling them. Move them to a "holding spot" and make a note on your calendar to revisit the box in three to six months. This will provide more peace as you process and more time to decide what you want to keep or donate. It will also help you to see if your children ask for the items again or if once, they are tucked away, they are forgotten about. (Moving things out of your primary spaces can be a great way to reveal what's missed or forgotten.) If your child receives lots of gifts from loved ones, it may be helpful to have a conversation with the gift-giver. Share with them how the "extras" aren't helping you with your minimization. A gift of an experience or a memory made together can often mean even more than another toy. Navigating these situations can be challenging, but done in love, it can have a tremendous impact. If toys and excess gifts are creating more stress for you, then make a point to address it.

There are many ways to set up your systems. So, after you have followed the six methods ensure to also apply these practices. These are my tips and tricks that, trust me, I have learned from experience!

- Place toys or any item that needs an extra layer of security up high or out of reach: Play-Doh, slime, paints, puzzles, games with millions of pieces, scissors, permanent markers, choking hazards, any kit with lots of parts or glitter. Always hide the glitter!

- Create zones and use storage that can be closed and/or has solid fronts. I love using a dresser for toys or a cube system with bins. You can loosely categorize items so kids can put things away easily (like with like), and it also creates a more cleaned-up look. When the drawers are closed, or the bins are placed back in the cubbies, the space returns to a sense of calm.

- Intentional toys mean more. Kids love to play, but play doesn't need to be complicated. Study what your children love to do and then foster those activities. There's a reason most kids play with a big appliance box—it allows them to be creative. Less is more when it comes to toys too!

Don't make play harder for your children than it needs to be. Lighten up their toy inventory levels and watch their freedom of expression and natural play expand! Kids don't need to be burdened with too much clutter or overloaded with choices. They will use more of their imagination and learn how to focus better when they do not feel overwhelmed.

A similar playroom/homeschool room I got to help organize for a young family.

Whichever recreational room you organized, keep play a priority! We all can benefit from working less and playing more.

Best Playroom Organizing Products

- Bins of all shapes and sizes help to contain and categorize.

- Picture or word labels are helpful for kids to know what things go where.

- Tall laundry baskets/hampers with lids make excellent storage solutions for stuffed animals or larger categories of toys. They are both pretty and practical!

- Put board games on a bookshelf, corral pool supplies in an outdoor storage container, and gather all sports balls in a net.

- Exercise racks work well to organize things by size and style.

- Use vertical space to hold play items up off the floor; this is both practical and pretty.

Work Zone

If you do any form of production at home, define this space and let's get it organized! This may be your home office where you work your remote job and then in the evenings shift to your hobby of photography. Or perhaps you are an avid crafter and have a room designated to all your quilting and sewing projects. Your space can be singular or it may have multiple purposes; just ensure there is division and order between the different tasks. In shared spaces try to keep your zones to only a few. This will depend on the size of your space and the things you work on but work to keep things simpler versus more complicated. Complicating things doesn't help with maintaining spaces. If we design a room and eight things take place in the space, then things can quickly get chaotic because so many things are happening in one room at one time.

Workspaces benefit from boundaries. Strategize to set up boundaries in the ways you need to. For example, in my home office I keep my doors open most of the time, but when I need to hop on a call or have a meeting, I put a sign up on my door. The sign says, "Please do not disturb. I'm on a call, thanks!" This creates a clear gatekeeper. Nobody (usually) enters except for the cat because she can't read, and she can also open doors. She's gifted and persistent.

After you have culled and categorized everything in your workspace then consider what additional containment and/or labels may help you to better organize things. What items are in your office or work room that don't belong? Return them to their rightful homes. Your workplace should not be a form of a drop zone! (Unless the items dropped are things that pertain to your work, hobby, or craft.) If you are visual—Bolts and Circles—you will want to design your storage systems so things are more on display and not tucked away and out of sight.

A simple tool to help with this space is to write out what things are currently running well in the space. What areas might need adjusting? Pivoting and redefining things can create an entirely new look and feel for your space. Commit to making things more organized by streamlining and simplifying. A more organized office will make it easier for you to be more productive.

This is also an important time to ask yourself if you are still passionate about working on the different tasks or hobbies you have set up in your room. I'm not talking about your job; my hope is that you like your job enough! I'm referring to knowing when you need to let something go. For example, as much as I want to practice piano, I don't. So why am I holding onto an electric keyboard? Is it time for me to let it go and accept what is? Or am I going to get to that pile of photo projects that I've been collecting for years to "work on"? Should I consider paring down my project list and being more realistic with what I can get to and/or will do?

It can be hard to focus and do deep work especially if you have too much in front of you. Streamline where you can and simplify. Identify what helps you to be productive and then set up your space(s) in those ways. It's your workspace; make it work for you. (See what I did there?)

Best Workspace Organizing Products

- Furniture pieces (desks, bookshelves, consoles) that have ample space and division will help you to put things away that do not need to be left out.

- A paper in-out/file system is essential! Paper needs a place to land when it comes into your home or office.

- Try to stick to only using one type of system for your to-dos (notepad, sticky note, or electronic list).

Chapter 14
Sleeping

"Tomorrow belongs to those who prepare for it today."

—African proverb

Before you read Part 1—Organizing Shapes—you might have thought I would tell you that you must make your bed every morning. Because this is what organized people do! It is an essential practice if you want to live more organized and have an organized home and life. But now that we've been together for a while you know I don't believe this to be true! If you like making your bed and it makes you feel better, then by all means, prioritize it and make it a daily habit. Or if you are more like me, feel free to let it go. You can be selective with what you choose to organize and how detailed you dive into organizing your spaces. Also work to say, *"Let it go!"* when you are decluttering and editing. It's freeing to sing with gusto and claim riddance of those items that are no longer adding to your life. Don't stay stuck by not letting go of what needs to be released.

However, the one thing you do need to hold onto is your commitment to getting adequate sleep. Sleep is incredibly vital to your health and well-being. So, as we turn toward your sleeping space—your bedroom—we will chat about why this room and your dedication to good rest needs to be protected at all costs.

My friend and fellow organizing expert Jessica Litman shared with me on my podcast that this is the room where she tells people to start to organize first. She believes your bedroom sets a tone for your mood, sleep, and energy levels. I don't disagree. This room can be a good place to begin. Resetting and organizing your bedroom will make it easier for you to rest, relax, and get quality sleep. If your bedroom is overrun with stuff and you don't feel a sense of calm, prepare to make a change!

Like every other space, work through the methods and be discerning with what you will keep in your bedroom. If you need to have other purposes for your bedroom, clearly define those pieces and create separation where you can. Your sleeping space is one where having less will help you to unwind with less effort. Think of a spa. What makes you relax when you walk into one? Usually, your five senses are influenced. You hear quiet and calming music and smell beautifully scented candles. Also cater to your senses in your bedroom. Clear your nightstands of things that don't belong. Minimize technology and distractions. Invest in nice linens and layers of coziness. Add a sound maker or darkening shades to help with unwanted noise or lights. When you implement intentional design and organization in your bedroom it will then create a ripple effect. Small changes will add up to big results. Think through the choices of your colors and decor. Are your selections adding to a sense of retreat and renewal? Could you make some adjustments to better enhance the space or create more of an oasis? What pieces add to the sense of calm and what things distract? Take notice and adjust.

Arrows and Diamonds, you might have a harder time shifting into rest mode. Examine what you can do to make your bedroom more of a haven. How can you help to create more separation from your production and work? Circles and Bolts, you might find resting easier to do, but be intentional about which gadgets or items you bring into your sleeping space. Your bedroom should remain focused on the top priority for the space: sleeping.

Your sleeping space is one where you want to have less.

Consider this: if you begin with organizing your bedroom would this then energize and inspire you to work to organize the other spaces in your home? Would your tomorrow be more peaceful and rest-filled if you could lie down on your pillow tonight and feel relaxed? How would you feel in the morning if you could sleep more deeply and not wake up surrounded by piles of clutter? If things have unraveled in your sleeping space, work to put things back together. One section and one zone at a time.

Best Bedroom Organizing Products

- Trays or baskets on nightstands help to define the tabletop and group things together.

- Select nightstands that have drawers and/or closed fronts to tuck things away.

- If you have a TV or electronics in your bedroom, create a spot to hold the remotes.

- Create a charging station, perhaps outside of your bedroom, to help keep technology and blue lights out of your sleeping zone.

- A basket of books or magazines can say, "Sit and relax."

- Be intentional with scale, furniture placement, and colors.

I snapped this picture of our dear friend's "charging station." This is a great way to corral all the technology in an organized and styled way. Their charging station here is in their living room; you could do this in any room.

Part IV
ORGANIZING STRATEGIES

"ORGANIZING THE HOME: 1 PERCENT BUYING BOXES AND BINS AND PUTTING STUFF AWAY. 99 PERCENT MOTIVATION."

—Anonymous

My intention is to be your organizing cheerleader. Like a best friend who will be direct and honest with you, but gentle too. I wanted to be a cheerleader in high school and despite trying out not once but twice for the team, I learned it wasn't meant to be. So, here's to second and third chances! Let's go, team; let's get organized!

It's time to talk strategy. Strategy refers to devising a plan of action to achieve something. This is why you picked up this book. You wanted to make a change. You were tired of feeling overwhelmed. You didn't know where to start. My hope is when you put this book down you will feel motivated and equipped to make the changes you want and need to make.

You now know your organizing shape and what that means to you and how you organize. We have peeled back the organizing onion, the seven common snags that get in our way of living organized—obstacles of preferences, values, schedules, experiences, purchases, memories, and abilities. These layers helped us to better understand why we get stuck. Then we shifted to the organizing systems that help us to organize the different spaces in our homes. We will now go even deeper into the "how to." You will learn the organizing tools you must sharpen and use. You will discover the critical piece of why managing your time intentionally is essential. You will recognize that tenacity trumps everything.

> **Strategy refers to devising a plan of action to achieve something.**

Tools

We all need a good tool belt when we take on a task. Organizing work is no exception. Here are the tools I recommend. These will help you to better focus and manage tasks. If you are navigating organizing with a neurodivergent condition, these tools are applicable to you too. I encourage you to try the different tools and see which ones work well for *you*. It often takes picking up and trying different options to discover the right tool for the project. Again, these are not "rules" but ideas and suggestions. You will decide what's effective. Trial and error are part of the process. Keep your aim in mind and your eye on the prize—an organized space.

Scope

Identify the scope of your project and plan. A plan will move you toward the result you want to achieve. Be specific and realistic. Both are incredibly important. For example, say you want to reorganize your pantry. You would state your aim is for it to be a space where everything has a home. More specifically, you can see all your inventory immediately and keep the space reset on a weekly basis. Specificity is important. If you do not know where you want to go, it will be difficult to stay the course. Keep in mind the importance of the size, scale, and scope of your project. I know it can be hard to know where to start and you can feel as though you want to get everything organized all at once. Avoid going too big. Smaller and concise is better. You will realize more small wins and your momentum will be positively affected. Scaling appropriately will help you to stay more focused and minimize getting pulled in different directions.

Schedule

The one predictable thing is that nothing is predictable. Therefore, if you want to make changes and get things organized, you must carve out time on your schedule. Our tendency is to move organizing tasks further down our to-do lists because other things scream louder at us. Your dishwasher needs to be unloaded, the car is due for an oil change, and the pets need to be taken to their vet appointments.

Work to schedule your organizing tasks as if they are appointments on your calendar. This is why my organizing sessions with clients are productive. We have blocked off a set amount of time. Distractions are minimized and work is prioritized. If you are more easily distracted or have lots of interruptions, consider how you can best set up your time for productivity. Imagine what forty-five minutes of zero interruptions would look like. How could you create this window of time? What steps do you need to take to facilitate this? When you have the time allotted, then you must commit to staying on task, focusing on the singular task in front of you. I tell myself to stay focused. I have an inner dialogue that encourages me to finish putting away my laundry or tells me to take five minutes and water all the houseplants. Let your inner voice be your inner cheerleader.

If you do not schedule or prioritize time to organize, I can guarantee you that you won't get to it. Sorry, that didn't sound cheerleader-like. But it's true! Organizing is a task that can be more easily ignored because it doesn't necessarily have the same time sensitivities. You then must choose to make it time-sensitive. Block smaller amounts of time so you can fit them in on your calendar, and this will also help you to stay more focused. Organizing is often something that gets pushed to the back burner. If this is your reality, then you must commit to scheduling the time to do the work.

Support

If you need help, ask. This can be a professional or a friend, whoever will step into the mess with you and hold you accountable. There is strength in knowing when you are stuck and identifying when you could benefit from help. Teamwork does make the dream work! Outsourcing and delegating are also great tools to implement. Be pragmatic about your strengths and then call on others to help by using their strengths.

Selective

Are you ready for a game-changing tool? You don't have to organize *everything*. You can have spaces or spots where things are more chaotic or less organized. Define this for you. This is again my example of not making my bed, but I could also apply this to my "project drawer," the one that is overly crowded or my car that is consistently a hot mess. It is fine to have areas where you don't overly organize, or you choose to keep things more macro-zoned. Adopting this attitude can be freeing. It allows you to let *some* things go. Playroom a mess on the daily because your kids are "playing"? Let it go. Shoes can't seem to make it into the designated "shoe basket"? It's okay. Pick up what matters and let the rest go. Just like we need to let go of our stuff we also need to release some of our expectations and standards. It is life-giving to embrace the mess (when required or when allowed) and then to keep focused on the systems that benefit you and are needed.

Part IV: Organizing Strategies

This is how my car regularly looks. I am constantly taking items to the donation center (and often my dogs like to join). Applying the "one in, one out" guideline is necessary to keeping a decluttered home.

Simplify

This is a big word that sounds simple enough, but it's not! Simplifying requires dedication. Here are some ways to simplify. We've already addressed the importance of decluttering and editing. This alone can change the trajectory of your spaces. I cannot emphasize this enough. I see many people drowning in their stuff and feeling the weight of their belongings. Our stuff should add to our lives, not subtract. Be ruthless where you can, and you will feel the results! Then implement any form of automation you can. This could be grocery delivery, setting up automatic payments, signing up for digital receipts or statements, or scheduling every next appointment on the spot. Think of simplifying as fewer steps. It's working smarter, not harder.

Sight

I'm using the word "sight" to mean two things. One, ask yourself what you want to *see* in your space. How much do you want on your surfaces? What is your clutter bandwidth? Where do you want less? Define the vision for your space. Secondly, keep things in sight for you where it benefits you. Bolts and Circles will want to have more open forms of storage and bins that are clear and/or labeled. Arrows and Diamonds might put too much out of sight, even if it's neatly organized. Stuff that isn't needed anymore put away in an organized fashion is still extra stuff you don't need. Keeping it real.

Courtney is a dear client of mine and I wanted her to share some of her story with you. She learned how to get more organized with an ADHD diagnosis and as a new mom. The tips she shares can help anyone with a neurodivergent condition.

> *I had always known I struggled with working memory, focus, and motivation for certain tasks. I struggled with organizing my thoughts, plans, and spaces in my life, despite being quite driven and successful both academically and professionally. I had always been able to overcome the struggle with enough drive, although it was draining because of the inefficiency caused by my disorganized, chaotic life and surroundings. I developed some very complicated coping mechanisms and accomplished a lot of things just before a deadline. I realized I needed some help organizing when I was pregnant with my daughter and I was completely overwhelmed by an "office" that had never been used as an office, a.k.a. "a room full of boxes full of office junk" and "baby stuff" that needed to become a functional baby nursery in only a few months. I knew if this didn't happen, my life could become literally unbearable, so it was crucial I figured something out.*
>
> *This is why organization specific to individuals with ADHD is so important. Through the organizing process, I could tell that Morgan had to adjust how*

*she helped me organize. She asked lots of questions about how I thought I would use the space and the items in the space, and I had to really think about it and imagine my thought process and how it would most likely play out, not my idealized version of how it would play out. For example, I would love to be the type of person who could have everything perfectly folded and tucked Marie Kondo–style, or stacked beautifully on a shelf. However, through an honest process, I know my ideal style is **visual and casual organization** where I am most likely to put the thing away where it generally goes because it is **easy** and promotes no chaos.*

Morgan had to do a ton of redirecting with me to keep me on task. This really was the beginning of me realizing how unique I was in my astonishing lack of focus and how real it was. She was gentle but firm and when I found out how much I could accomplish when I was forced to stay on task, I was so excited. Using an organizer for just a few hours at a time became a game-changer because if I had scheduled the time, I could not procrastinate. I had a huge dopamine hit at the end of our organizing sessions when I saw how much I accomplished!

*At that time, I started to suspect I had an ADHD brain, but it wasn't until I had my baby that I really started to not be able to cope. I began watching YouTube channels by ADHD moms and they were echoing my experience of feeling like my world was caving in. Babies do not accommodate our complicated coping mechanisms and inefficiency and disorganization is already a given with sleep deprivation. Thank goodness I had learned some organizing skills **before** the baby came! I finally got a much-needed diagnosis (at age thirty-five), which helped me to name the monster, validate my struggles, and reassure me I was on the right path to help. I started devouring content on life skills for ADHD brains and being a mom with executive dysfunction. I finally felt more accepting of my limitations, and rather than pushing my brain to work harder, I now accept that it struggles with certain things and if I organize a certain way, I can set myself up for things to be easier.*

*Because ADHD affects our executive function, organizing with us needs to really focus on alleviating our need to rely on our working memory. **This means lots of labels on everything!** Even if it seems obvious. Because it lets your brain relax a little and move a little faster. Also, it's important for us to have all the items to accomplish a task in the same place. So, for instance,* *keeping the dog food and treats and medicine in a container near the dog bowls. Keeping your workout shoes and clothes/ bras/socks together in the closet or set of drawers (this was like a lightbulb for me!), rather than keeping them separate with categories of socks, pants, shoes, bras, etc.*

*It's important I keep things **I use in sight and not put away**. I'm working on making things look aesthetically pleasing while being out in plain sight. It's hard because I have always been taught that this looks cluttered, but the other way just doesn't work for me and leads to actual clutter anyway.*

Time Management

I hope these two words don't irritate you. I wrote an entire book on managing your time because I feel so passionately about it. Our time is a gift and I hope you can use your time wisely and effectively to live how you want to live. On that note, I'll assume we're on the same page. Well, we are because you are reading this page. Ha! What I mean is you want to live with less. You want to spend less time picking things up and putting them away. You are craving more time for slowness and making memories. If this is true for you then let's get to the core of how you manage your time. Time management is the foundation of an organized home. We all have the same number of hours in each day to do what is before us; what we then must decide is what we will do with our time.

As I shared previously, organization takes a combination of both time and motivation. Most of the time, these two things are not aligned. You must recognize where you can affect these two tools. How can you create or carve out more time to do organizing work? Where could you delegate some tasks to others to free your time to reset things? Why are you unmotivated? What can you do to help you be more motivated to create change? Do you want to organize your space(s)? Is something not as important to you as it is to someone else? There is no perfect harmony, but identifying why these two pieces can be at odds for you is essential to making progress. I love the quote by Denzel Washington: *"Do what you have to do, to do what you want to do."* This sums up prioritization perfectly.

On a gentle note, be kind to yourself. Perhaps your life season is full, and you are barely getting through each day. You know your capacities and abilities. Choose to then focus on the highest priorities only. Shift everything lower that you can. Realistic strategies are the best tools you can grab at this moment.

There are no magic answers here when it comes to how to best align these two things. You must get to your core and find the motivation. This begins with checking in and asking what is of highest importance and where you can be more selective with your organization. Lightening your load is a great tool to choose too! I'll finish my "time talk" with this. *If* something is important to you, then make it important. If it's not important to you, then say that. Name it and claim it. There is freedom in being decisive.

Tenacity

Tenacity means you keep trying until you reach your goal. You keep going; you stay committed. Easier said than done. This makes me think of childbirth, running a marathon, or writing a book. All things I've done that I wasn't sure I could or would make it through. It's hard work to see something to completion, especially if it's a time-intensive project. Organizing takes tenacity. When someone calls me and says they want to get their entire home organized and wanted it done yesterday, I chuckle to myself. Disorganization takes place over time. Things unravel piece by piece and likewise they need to be picked up again—piece by piece. To get things reorganized it's a slow and steady process. And if done in a methodical and intentional way, it is more likely to be done to completion. I like to say, "Pace your race!"

If you are working to organize a large space or several parts in your home, treat the process like a marathon versus a sprint. This goes back to the step-by-step methodology. When you work in smaller steps, it will equate to greater long-term progress. Choosing to be tenacious will help you to realize your potential.

You are good at organizing. Believe in yourself and know yourself. Organize how it works for you to organize and stay the course. I'm cheering you on!

Conclusion

Your Habits

"You can't read about push-ups. You gotta do 'em."
—Gary Vaynerchuk

Conclusion: Your Habits

We've all heard it takes twenty-one days to form a habit. However, according to a study[8] the time range can span anywhere from eighteen days to over two hundred and fifty days! The average length of time hovers around sixty-six days. That's two months of committing and practicing a new way of doing something. Consider this as we talk about the importance of habit-building.

You can go through and touch every single item in your home. You can follow the Morganizing Methods and get every space reorganized, but this does not mean you will *stay* organized. You must also develop healthy organizing habits—choices you commit to, like intentional shopping and scheduling time to reset your spaces. It is practicing the deliberate art of bringing in one item in and taking one item out. Identify homes for your household items, ensuring everything is stored *like with like*. It means making cleaning up and tidying both parts of your daily routine.

Go back to the kindergarten classroom. We all know how a simple system looks and works. This is the same application I want you to take home with you. Simplify everywhere you can. The health benefits of living more organized are numerous. When you develop good organizational habits, you will save yourself time, money, energy, stress, and more. Whereas, when you are disorganized, the results are the opposite. I want you to stay off the disorganization hamster wheel. And I know you can!

Start small with your organizing habits. Every step you take toward efficiency and organization will add up. Set a timer for five minutes and make yourself focus on getting through one section or space. Elect to receive one bill/statement electronically. Shop with a list or don't shop (try using things you already own). Recycle or throw things away immediately upon use. When you are headed upstairs or downstairs, or in or out, take item(s) with you and put them away.

Your home should be your haven, a relief from stress, not the cause of stress. I challenge you to take the next sixty-six days and commit to building three organizing habits into your home and life. Honor your organizing shape and the snags that get in your way. Apply *good enough* systems and use

---

8   Lally, Phillippa. "How are Habits Formed?" *European Journal of Social Psychology.* onlinelibrary.wiley.com/doi/abs/10.1002/ejsp.674.

intentional strategies to help you not only get organized but stay organized. You can do this, one step at a time.

As James Clear says, *"Ultimately, it is your commitment to the process that will determine your progress."* Commit to moving from *aspiration to action*. Don't just read about how to do it; go do it!

Organizing Habits:

1. _____

2. _____

3. _____

Acknowledgements

Beginning with my family, Tribe Tyree—in alphabetical order, of course.

Ainsley: you are my mini-me in so many ways and yet, so different and unique too. I absolutely adore you. Thank you for being my sounding board, helping me with my business, and asking me to help you with organizing your stuff. You know it makes my heart happy!

Berkley: you always pay me the nicest compliments that I don't take for granted! I can't begin to tell you what a light you are in our family. *You* spark joy! Your energy, enthusiasm, and empathy are all traits I admire. As you leave the nest, Dad and I are always here for you, cheering you on every step of the way.

Connor: you couldn't be a cooler person if you tried. Most everything you attempt turns into success. I am proud of you, son, for being self-aware, knowing your boundaries, and loving others incredibly deeply. Watching your take on life and spirit for adventure energizes me.

David: you are my home. Thank you for always supporting me in all my crazy endeavors! You encourage me to go for my dreams and then help to equip me along the way. My work is only successful because of you. Sharing this life with you and raising our family has been the absolute best. As we enter our next season and chapter, I can't wait to see what is to come.

Family, Friends, Clients

Mom and Dad: you taught me everything I know. Thank you for leading me toward such a solid path in life. Your examples of faith, friendship, and follow through have been the biggest blessings of all.

Haley: my sister, my friend. Thank you for always helping me behind the scenes and being so willing to jump in and help share my message. I have such a deep respect for you and who you are. Love you, sis!

Tiffany: you light up this world and have been such a gift to me. Thank you for being so enthusiastic, encouraging, and fun! Our walks and talks are my favorite.

Kristen: thank you for being my business sounding partner, and someone I can always be authentic with. Your art of snapping such beautiful moments of me and my family is a precious gift!

Julie: your friendship means so much to me. It's as if you are more my sister than my friend. Our late-night chats in Paris and random morning phone calls always bring a big smile to my face.

Brandy: I'm so thankful you reached out and joined the MWM team. The saddest part is that it wasn't long enough! You were there when I needed help most and it's been a pleasure working alongside you.

Ryan, Stacey, Shannon, Erika, Bill, Tiffany, Debbie, Andy, Rachel, Shelly, Josh & Michele, Courtney, Kendra, Willie & Sarah, Carrie, Katie, Amy, Crystal, Ainsley, and Mom and Dad—thank you for allowing me to share your stories and/or pictures. I so appreciate that you trusted me to share a slice of your story and welcomed me into your homes.

Mango Team

It takes an incredible team to write this many words and get them printed, marketed, and distributed. Thank you, Mango, for allowing me to help others experience more peace and calm in their homes. It is because of you and your support that this book came to be.

About the Author

Morgan Tyree, also known as "The Morganizer," is the author of *Take Back Your Time*, *Your Hospitality Personality*, and *The Productivity Zone*. For the past decade she has been encouraging and equipping homeowners to take back their homes. As a professional organizer she is the master of coaching organizational systems. Part counselor, part comedian (people tell her she is funny), she delicately guides her clients and readers on how to navigate the stressors surrounding home organization.

Tyree received her degree in Business Management-Entrepreneurship from the University of Oregon (go Ducks!) and has a former corporate background working in the fields of management, marketing, and human resources. A self-proclaimed people person, she considers it a privilege to walk with others on their path to self-improvement.

Morgan lives with her husband, David, in the Colorado Front Range where they are settling in as empty nesters. When she is not organizing, writing, or strolling through Target (with a chai tea in hand), she can likely be found teaching group exercise classes. This long-time hobby job of hers began over thirty years ago and she just can't quit. Mostly because she gets to wear a microphone and tell jokes!

Mango Publishing, established in 2014, publishes an eclectic list of books by diverse authors—both new and established voices—on topics ranging from business, personal growth, women's empowerment, LGBTQ studies, health, and spirituality to history, popular culture, time management, decluttering, lifestyle, mental wellness, aging, and sustainable living. We were named 2019 *and* 2020's #1 fastest growing independent publisher by *Publishers Weekly*. Our success is driven by our main goal, which is to publish high-quality books that will entertain readers as well as make a positive difference in their lives.

Our readers are our most important resource; we value your input, suggestions, and ideas. We'd love to hear from you—after all, we are publishing books for you!

Please stay in touch with us and follow us at:

Facebook: Mango Publishing
Twitter: @MangoPublishing
Instagram: @MangoPublishing
LinkedIn: Mango Publishing
Pinterest: Mango Publishing
Newsletter: mangopublishinggroup.com/newsletter

Join us on Mango's journey to reinvent publishing, one book at a time.